The BIG 6™

The Definitive Big6™ Workshop Handbook

THIRD EDITION

by

MICHAEL B. EISENBERG
ROBERT E. BERKOWITZ

Linworth
PUBLISHING, INC

Library of Congress Cataloging-in-Publication Data

Eisenberg, Michael.
The definitive Big6 workshop handbook / by Michael B. Eisenberg and Robert E. Berkowitz.-- 3rd ed.
p. cm.
Rev. ed. of: The new improved Big6 workshop handbook. c1999.
Includes bibliographical references and index.
ISBN 1-58683-159-3 (pbk.)
1. Information retrieval--Study and teaching. 2. Information retrieval--Study and teaching--United States. 3. Electronic information resource literacy--Study and teaching. 4. Electronic information resource literacy--Study and teaching--United States. I. Title: Definitive Big 6 workshop handbook. II. Title: Definitive Big six workshop handbook. III. Berkowitz, Robert E. IV. Eisenberg, Michael. New improved Big6 workshop handbook. V. Title.
ZA3075.E4 2003
025.5'24'071--dc22

2003018515

Published by Linworth Publishing, Inc.
480 East Wilson Bridge Road, Suite L
Worthington, Ohio 43085-2372

ISBN: 1-58683-159-3

5 4 3

Table of Contents

List of Worksheets

The Big6™ Foreword

Welcome Big6er's all—present and future!

We are excited to offer you this third edition of the Big6™ Workshop Handbook.

Our previous handbook was successfully used all over the world as a guide for Big6™ professional development workshops and self-study to help teacher-librarians, classroom teachers, administrators, and parents learn the Big6™ approach. This edition of the workbook includes new and revised worksheets, answers to training exercises, Super3, resources, and explanations on how to use the various materials in Big6™ training contexts. We have included a new chapter that discusses the Big6™ within teaching and learning contexts. All together, *The Definitive Big6™ Handbook* focuses on learning about, using, and teaching the Big6™ Skills approach to information and technology skills.

The Definitive Big6™ Workshop Handbook is written to help classroom teachers, teacher-librarians, technology teachers, administrators, parents, community members, and students to do the following:

- Learn about the Big6™
- Use the Big6™ process in their own activities, personal, educational, and business, and
- Implement a Big6™ approach to information and technology skills in classrooms, libraries, and labs; in individual schools and districts; in regions and states; and even as part of national and international initiatives.

Information and technology literacy are major concerns throughout our society in education, in business, and in our personal lives. There is widespread recognition that basic life skills for the 21st century are related to the use of information and technology. All people need the ability to identify information needs and then find, use, apply, and evaluate information for those needs.

At its most fundamental level, the Big6™ is a six-stage process model for information problem-solving and decision-making. We have spent the past 15 years working in public and private education, business, government, and communities to improve information problem-solving and technology skills. The Big6™ is widely recognized as a practical approach to the design and implementation of information and technology skills programs by integrating Big6™ Skills within subject area curriculum and in meaningful contexts.

The Big6™ is dedicated to helping people learn essential information and technology skills necessary for success. The publications and services surrounding the Big6™ approach include The *Big6™ eNewsletter*, books, journal articles, posters, cards, bookmarks, videos, the Big6™ listserv, and the Big6™ Web site for educators and parents (For more information on all of these resources and services, visit <www.big6.org>). Those involved with the Big6™ are really part of a "movement" that continues to gain momentum.

Part I, Part II, and Part III of the book help the reader identify the need for information and technology skills and develop a working understanding of the Big6™, Little 12, and Super3. Part IV concentrates on technology and how to use technology in a meaningful way through integration within the Big6™ framework. Part V turns to implementing the Big6™ on the micro (lesson and unit) level. Part VI offers specific approaches to assessment using the Big6™ steps, and Part VII shows the importance of collaboration and partnerships. Part VIII prepares readers to integrate Big6™ Skills with the curriculum by using curriculum-mapping techniques. The final sections of the book, Part IX and Part X, provide exercises for including parents and the school district (macro level) in the overall plan for success. Part XI contains important supplemental readings that support the Big6™ approach.

If you are discovering the Big6™ for the first time, this handbook will guide you through the basic concepts and give you a strategy for success. Our book is a good source of information about the Big6™ approach and how it can be implemented in your school. If you are already using the Big6™, this third edition will help you to expand your efforts. We encourage you to use *The Definitive Big6™ Workshop Handbook* to support local Big6™ professional development initiatives.

Remember to THINK BIG! What you do in terms of education and teaching essential information and technology skills is critically important to student success in school and in later life. Information literacy skills are not optional—they are basic skills for success in the 21st century. We hope this Workshop Handbook helps you effectively implement the Big6™ approach in information and technology literacy programs in your educational setting.

We love to hear from all Big6ers. Visit our Web site: <www.Big6.com>, or contact us directly at info@big6.com.

We would like to thank Sue Wurster, Joan Laskowski, Blythe Bennett, and Wendy Medvetz for their assistance in preparing this new edition. And, as always, thanks to our publisher, Marlene Woo-Lun, a truly unique and supportive person — it is a great joy to work with you.

Mike Eisenberg & Bob Berkowitz
Seattle, Washington, and Rochester, New York
May 1, 2003

About the Authors

MICHAEL B. EISENBERG

Mike Eisenberg is dean and professor of the Information School of the University of Washington. Under his direction, the School has transformed into a central player on campus, in the information field, and in the broader community with four degree programs (including distance offerings), an impressive research profile including 24 funded research projects, professional development and service course. Student enrollment has almost tripled in three years.

Prior to his role as Dean, Mike Eisenberg worked for many years as professor of information studies at Syracuse University and as Director of the Information Institute of Syracuse (which includes the ERIC Clearinghouse on Information & Technology, the award-winning AskERIC project, and GEM, the Gateway to Educational Materials). Mike and his co-author Bob Berkowitz created "the Big6" the most widely used approach to information literacy in K-12 education in the world. Mike has worked with thousands of students—preK through higher education as well as people in public schools, business, government, and communities—to gain an "information perspective" and improve their information and technology abilities. Mike has written numerous books and articles on aspects of information science, education, information literacy, library media work, and information technology.

Mike earned his Ph.D. in Information Transfer from the School of Information Studies at Syracuse University and his Master of Library Science from the State University of New York at Albany.

E-mail: Mike_Eisenberg@Big6.com

ROBERT E. BERKOWITZ

Bob is a strong believer in goals-oriented management, the library media specialist as a key partner in the excellence in education—effective schools movement, and the integration of critical thinking skills into library & information skills instruction. Putting these ideas into action, Bob acted as Library Media Specialist Consultant to a research skills-based English curriculum project that won National Council of Teachers of English recognition as a Center of Excellence in English and the Language Arts.

Bob is high school library media specialist and K-12 advisor for library and information services at Wayne Central Schools, (Ontario Center, NY), an Adjunct Instructor at Syracuse University's School of Information Studies, W.K. Kellogg Foundation Expert in Residence (12/2001), and Consultant to Mansfield State University's School

Library & Information Technologies graduate program. He is often requested to share his ideas in conferences and seminars.

Bob has collaborated with Mike Eisenberg to write: *Helping with Homework* (1996), *Teaching Information & Technology Skills: The Big6™ in Elementary Schools* (1999), *Teaching Information & Technology Skills: The Big6™ in Secondary Schools* (2000). Recently published interviews with Bob Berkowitz include: "Moving Every Child Ahead: The Big6™ Success Strategy," (May/June, 2002), *MultiMedia Schools*; and "Acing the Exam: How Can Librarians Boost Students' Test Scores?"(October, 2002), *School Library Journal.*

E-mail: Bob_Berkowitz@Big6.com

Part I: Introducing the Big6™

Introducing the Big6™

Introduction

All journeys begin with a first step. In some respects, taking that first step forward takes a certain degree of courage—especially when setting out on a new road. A new road represents change. Change. It is an idea that excites but at the same time can make us quite uncomfortable.

Planning for Change

In his workshops, Mike often starts with a Calvin and Hobbes cartoon about change. It's the one that shows Calvin and Hobbes coming down a hill in a wagon. Calvin says, "I thrive on change." Hobbes says, "You? You threw a fit this morning because your mom put less jelly on your toast than yesterday." Calvin then says, "I thrive on making other people change."

Education today is all about change. There are all kinds of new demands on teachers and students—some driven by environment and mandates—but the more profound demands are created by fundamental changes in our society, the information society. We live in an increasingly complex information world. Education—schools, teachers, caregivers—must come to grips with what knowledge and skills students really need and then make sure that students gain the needed knowledge and skills.

We can no longer rely on the old ways of doing things—a textbook, lecture, and test. Instead, we need to use a wide range of resources, guide and assist, and assess through a range of individual and collaborative projects. The information society demands that students need to find, use, and process a wide range of information, often in a very short period of time. Students learn these skills through guidance, teamwork, and projects. And, we assess their skills and knowledge by looking at the authentic results of their efforts.

Making these changes will not necessarily be easy, but it is vital that we do so. The materials in this chapter can help. The chapter is designed help you understand the nature of instructional change, how to overcome resistance to it, and how to approach others to make changes with you.

Number Connecting Exercise

The first activity in the Workshop Handbook—the Number Connecting Exercise—is designed to address people's natural aversion to change. As you and other participants go through this exercise, it becomes evident that shifts of focus or process are okay, healthy, and appropriate. Several elements must be in place in order to effect change. These elements include the following:

Compatibility: Compatible with current instructional practice
Complexity: Easy to understand and explain to others
Observability: Observable as change
Try-ability: Easy to try without taking a big risk

CCOT—that's one way to remember these aspects of creating change—CCOT.

Despite the complex look of this first activity, it satisfies the CCOT principles of change. Numbers, number recognition, and number sequencing are well-known skills among the vast majority of adults and children alike. Teachers often ask students to engage these kinds of skills (Compatibility). The exercise is simple to do even though there is a time constraint that adds to the challenge, and there are only two instructions (Complexity). The visual nature makes it easy for the participant to see what he or she has done, and whether the participant has changed his or her approach (Observability). All participants will feel comfortable trying this exercise; it minimizes risk factors that may inhibit a participant's willingness to engage in the task.

Potential risk factors include embarrassment, fear of failure, or lack of time. The participants do this activity on their own and are not required to share the results, thus eliminating the potential for embarrassment. There is no way for a participant to fail in the exercise because there are multiple opportunities to practice the skills, and each person will improve to some degree. Lastly, the activity takes only two and one-half to three minutes to complete, which effectively eliminates the excuse that trying the exercise will take too long (Try-ability).

Bob uses the Number Connecting Exercise to make some key points about change:

1. **Change:** Be careful not to get too complacent, or too comfortable. Change is just around the corner.
2. **Repetition:** We learn through repetition.

3. **Patterns:** There are patterns that we can learn to help us be effective and efficient.
4. **Shared experiences:** Sharing common experiences helps to bring people together.

The Number Connecting Exercise is our first introduction to change and the challenges facing students and educators. Following the Number Connecting Exercise is a handout of *PowerPoint* slides used to present a discussion about the challenges of the information society. We all know that the amount of available information is overwhelming. Our experience is that most people need a system for "sorting and sifting" all of this information. They also want a successful method for becoming efficient and effective information problem-solvers. That's the Big6™.

The *PowerPoint* slides offer a context for the Big6™ in terms of information literacy and information needs in our society. We also provide insights into the key role for library media specialists in ensuring that students gain the skills they need. Both of us come from a library media background. We are tireless supporters of an active, engaged role for teacher-librarians in collaborating with classroom teachers and others to provide meaningful, integrated Big6™ instruction.

We expect you to supplement these *PowerPoint* slides with slides of your own. You will have numerous opportunities to personalize your Big6™ presentation throughout this handbook, and we encourage you to do so. Think about the different audiences for the Big6™, and how you would customize your presentation of the information. Also consider how you will evaluate whether you were successful so that you can improve for the next time.

In summary, this first section introduces change and a new approach to thinking about (1) the skills and knowledge that students really need and (2) how to help students gain those skills and knowledge.

We believe that students must be effective and efficient information problem-solvers, and that we must change our schools and ourselves in order to help students succeed.

Number Connecting Exercise

Directions

Please do not turn the page until you are told to do so.

The next five pages are sheets of numbers. The numbers are scattered all over the page, but they are all there and it will be your job to find them. To get you started, the number one will always be found at the top left corner; it has a circle around it.

Use a pen to connect the numbers in order, beginning with number one, then two, then three, and so on. You should work as fast as you can because your goal is to connect as many numbers as possible. However, please note that:

1. You must begin with the number one and you cannot skip any numbers. Thus, you cannot connect 30 to 31 until you have already connected the previous 29 numbers.
2. Lines can cross. When you are done, there will not be a picture of anything.

There are five pages of numbers. You will be allotted 30 seconds per page. On each page, you must begin again with the number one. Work as fast as you can. You will be told when your time is up.

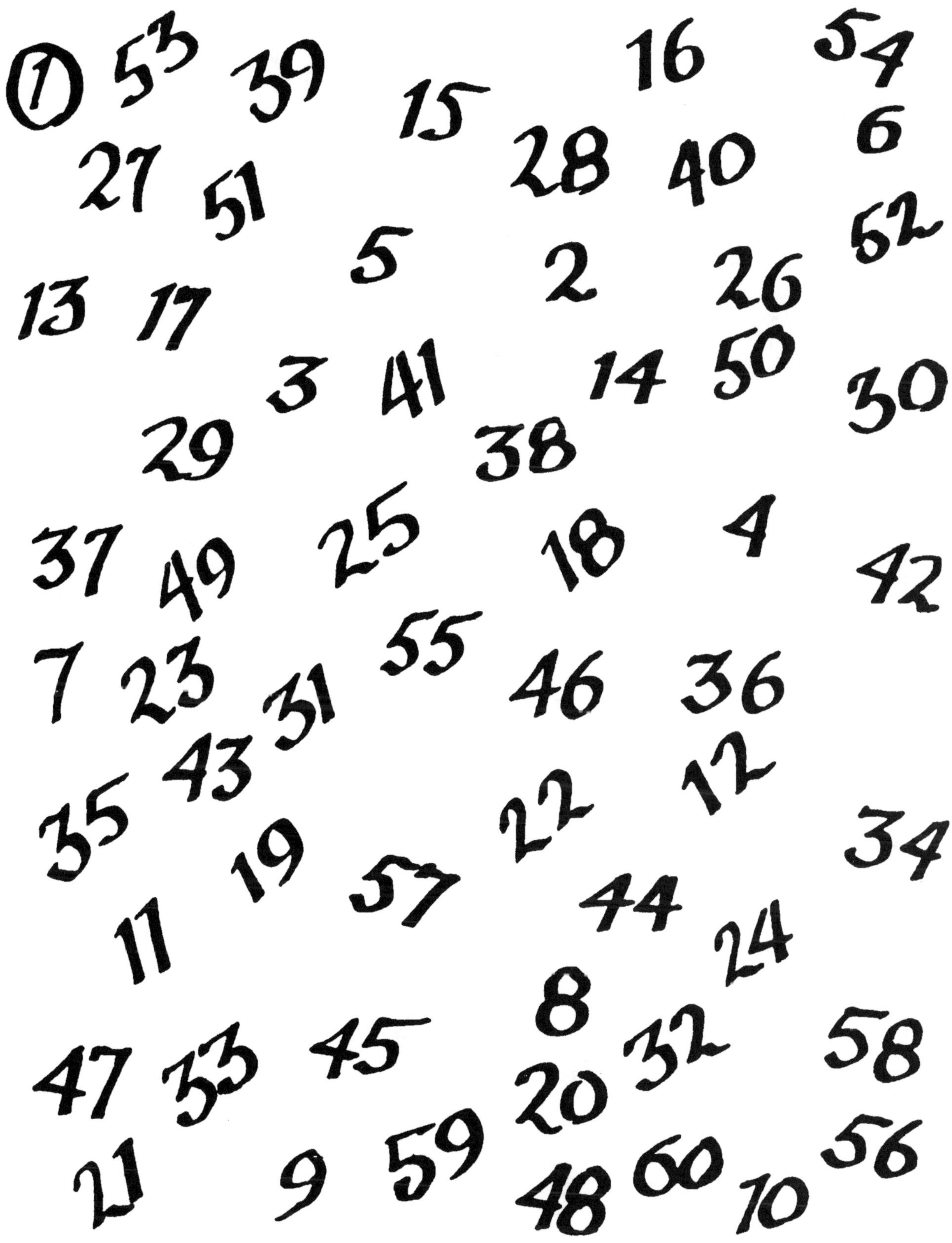
1
53
39
15
16
54
27
51
28
40
6
5
2
26
52
13
17
3
41
14
50
30
29
38
37
49
25
18
4
42
7
23
31
55
46
36
35
43
22
12
34
11
19
57
44
24
8
47
33
45
32
58
20
21
9
59
48
60
10
56

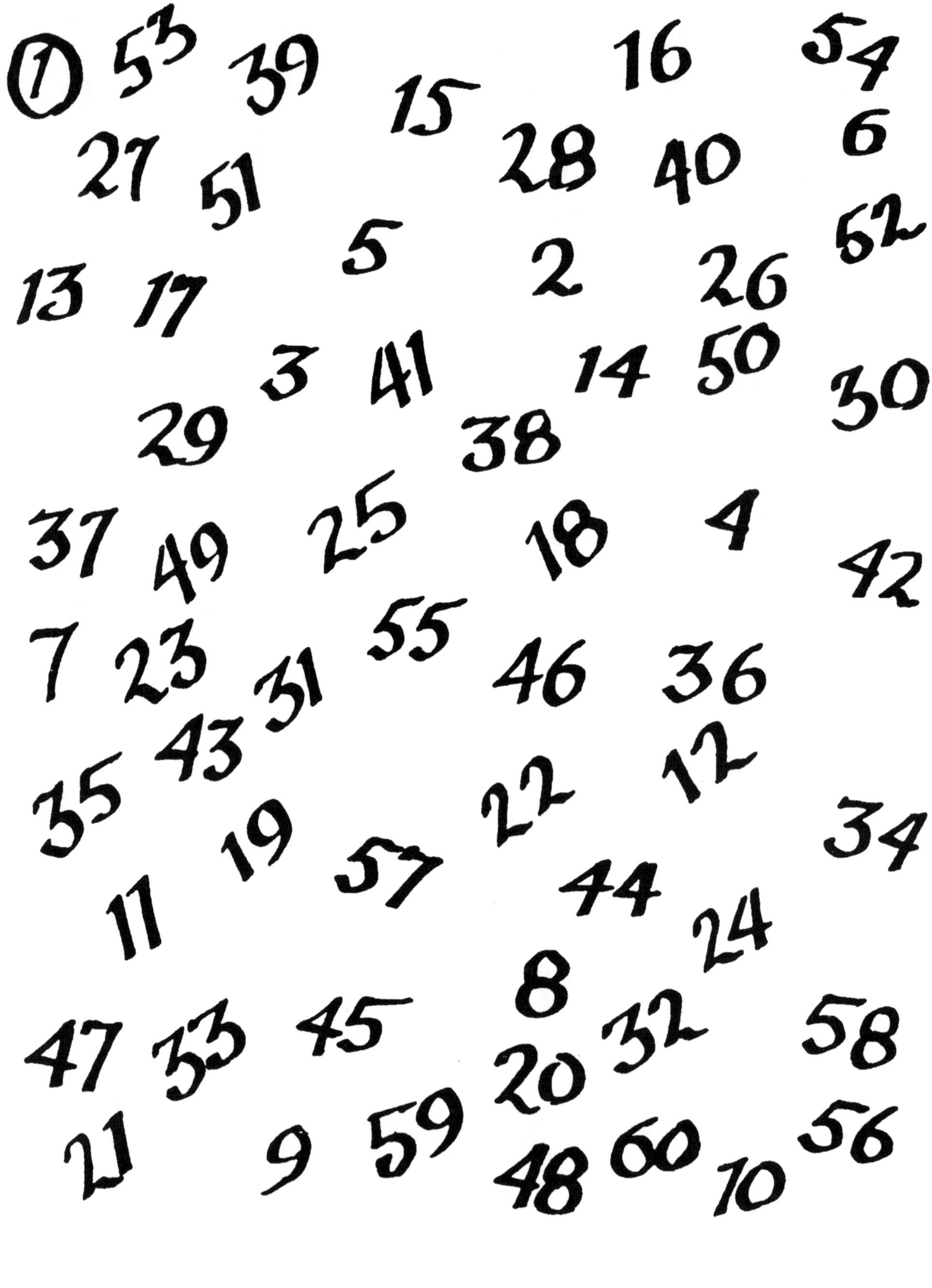
1 53 39 15 16 54
27 51 28 40 6
13 17 5 2 26 52
3 41 14 50 30
29 38
37 49 25 18 4 42
7 23 55 46 36
31 43 35 22 12
19 57 34
11 44 24
8
47 33 45 32 58
20
21 9 59 48 60 10 56

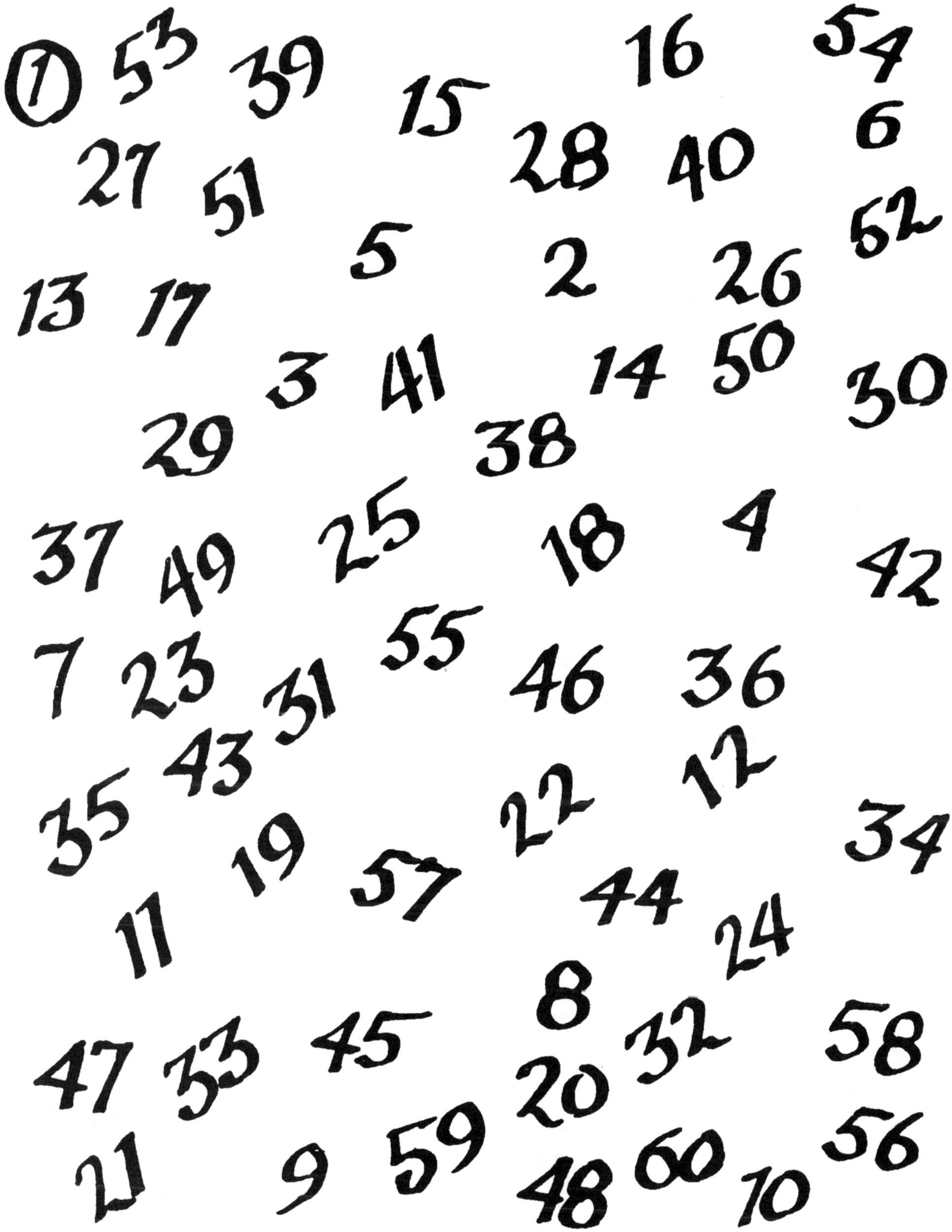
1 53 39 15 16 54
6
27 51 28 40
5 2 26 52
13 17 3 41 14 50 30
29 38
37 49 25 18 4 42
7 23 55 31 46 36
43 35 22 12 34
19 57 44
11 24
8
47 33 45 32 58
20
21 9 59 48 60 10 56

1
53
39
15
16
54
27
51
28
40
6
13
17
5
2
26
62
3
41
14
50
30
29
38
37
49
25
18
4
42
7
23
31
55
46
36
35
43
22
12
34
11
19
57
44
24
8
47
33
45
20
32
58
21
9
59
48
60
10
56

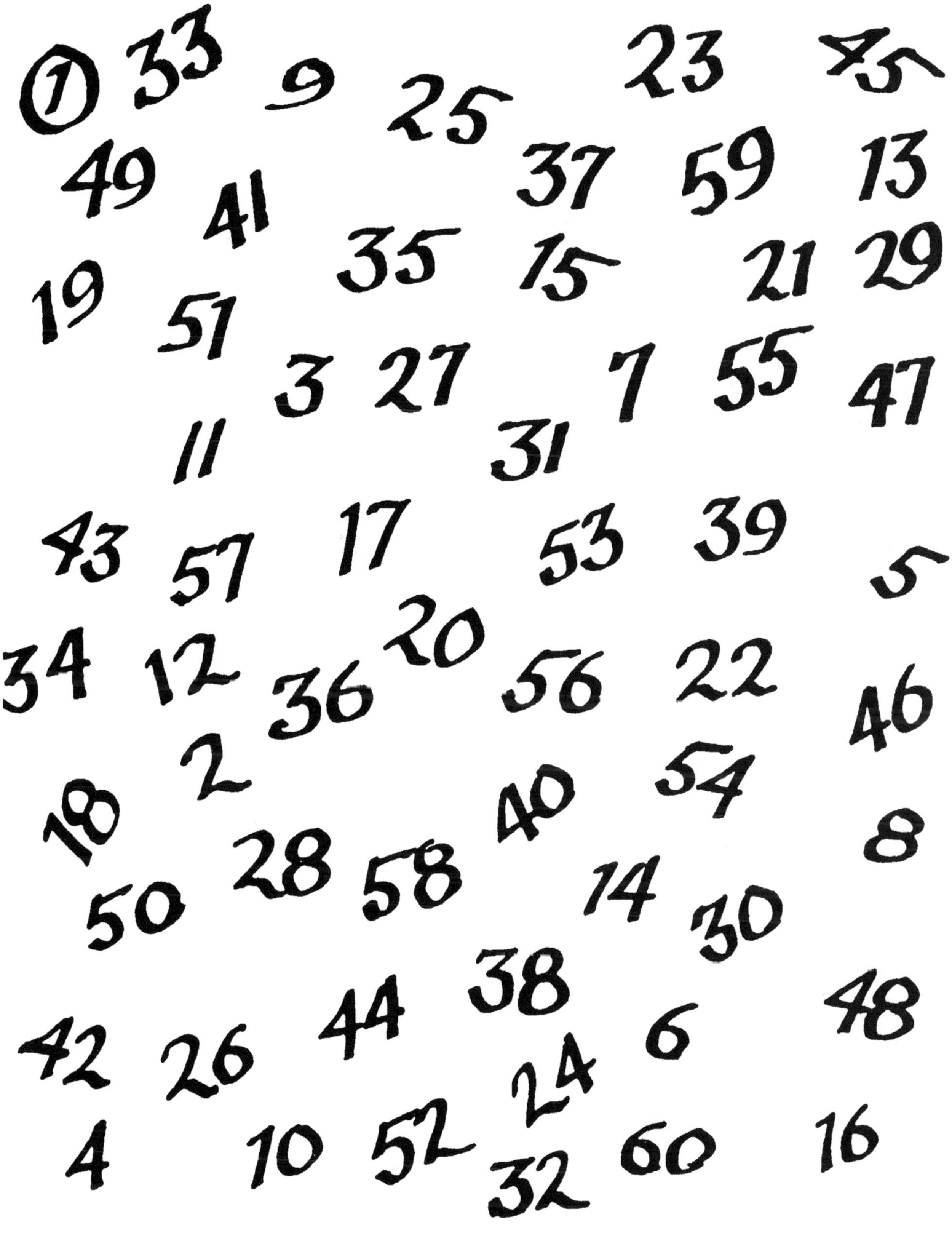
1 33 9 25 23 45
49 41 37 59 13
19 51 35 15 21 29
3 27 7 55 47
11 31
43 57 17 53 39 5
34 12 36 20 56 22 46
18 2 40 54 8
50 28 58 14 30
42 26 44 38 6 48 24
4 10 52 32 60 16

The Information Age: Implications for Learning and Teaching

Information Age — Problems

- Information overload
- Information quality
- Student lack of information & technology skills
- Technology out of context

Quality

"More than 2/3 of teens said within the last year that they use the Internet as their major resource when doing a big project for school..."

Lester, Will, "High School Students Love Net for Research," Syracuse Post Standard, 8/21/01 (from AP)

In a study of 500 sites used by Colorado high school students to do research, only 27% of the sites were judged to be reliable for academic research!

Ebersol, Samuel, "Uses and Gratifications of the Web among Students," *Journal of Computer-Mediated Communication*, 6(1): September 2000, <www.asusc.org/jcmc/vol6/issue1/ebersole.html>

Colhoun, Alexander. "But—I Found It on the Internet!" *Christian Science Monitor.* 25 April 2000: 16.

Information Overload

"Today, a daily *New York Times* has more printed information in it than a person would come across in an entire lifetime in the 17th Century."

David Lewis "Introduction to Dying for Information," <www.reuters.com/rbb/research/dfiforframe.htm>, 1996

The Solution?

- Discourage Web use?
- Filtering?

The Solution?

- Speed things up?
- Pack in more and more content?
- Add more technology?

Alternative Solution: Information Literacy

- Helping students to be discriminating users of information.
- Helping students learn to use essential information & technology skills in context.
- The Big6™.

Information Literacy

"To be information literate, a person must be able to recognize when information is needed and have the ability to locate, evaluate, and use effectively the needed information."

American Library Association, 1989

The Big6™ Skills

1. Task Definition
2. Info Seeking Strategies
3. Location & Access
4. Use of Information
5. Synthesis
6. Evaluation

Information Literacy

"Information literacy, the ability to locate, process and use information effectively, equips individuals to take advantage of the opportunities inherent in the global information society."

Assoc. for Supervision and Curriculum Dev., 1991

The Big6™ Information Problem-Solving Process

1. **Task Definition:**
   1.1 Define the problem.
   1.2 Identify the information needed.
2. **Information Seeking Strategies:**
   2.1 Determine all possible sources.
   2.2 Select the best sources.
3. **Location and Access:**
   3.1 Locate sources.
   3.2 Find information within sources.
4. **Use of Information:**
   4.1 Engage (e.g., read, hear, view).
   4.2 Extract relevant information.
5. **Synthesis:**
   5.1 Organize information from multiple sources.
   5.2 Present information.
6. **Evaluation:**
   6.1 Judge the result (effectiveness).
   6.2 Judge the process (efficiency).

The Super3

Imagine you are the main character in a story:

Beginning—Plan

Middle—Do

End—Review

Summary—Solutions

- Process as well as content.
- Information and technology literacy.
- Context—not an add-on!
  - ✓ within the process
  - ✓ technology in a Big6™ context
  - ✓ tied to existing curriculum instruction, and assignments

Themes of the Big6™

1. The Big6 process can be applied in all subjects, with students of all ages, and across all grade levels (K–20).
2. The Big6 is adaptable and flexible; it can be applied to any information situation.
3. Technology skills take on meaning within the Big6 process.
4. Using the Big6 is not always a linear, step-by-step process.
5. The Big6 process is necessary and sufficient for solving problems and completing tasks.
6. The Big6 is an ideal approach for integrating information literacy learning with all subject area curricula at all grade levels.

Explaining the Big6™

- Essential information skills
- A model of the problem-solving process
- Simple ... but not really
- Widely applicable
- Easy to implement
- Powerful

Notes:

The Big6™ Skills Approach to Information Problem-Solving

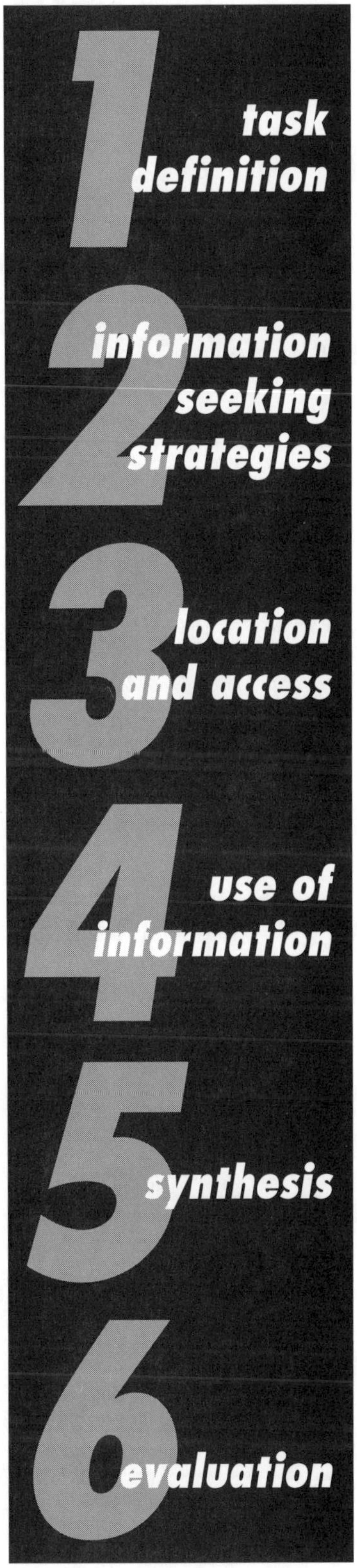

The Big6™ Skills

The Big6 is a process model of how people of all ages solve an information problem.

1. Task Definition

1.1 Define the information problem
1.2 Identify information needed to complete the task (to solve the information problem)
- What's the task?
- What types of information do I need?

2. Information Seeking Strategies

2.1 Determine the range of possible sources (brainstorm)
2.2 Evaluate the different possible sources to determine priorities (select the best sources)
- What are possible sources?
- Which are the best?

3. Location and Access

3.1 Locate sources (intellectually and physically)
3.2 Find information within sources
- Where is each source?
- Where is the information in each source?

4. Use of Information

4.1 Engage (e.g., read, hear, view, touch) the information in a source
4.2 Extract relevant information from a source
- How can I best use each source?
- What information in each source is useful?

5. Synthesis

5.1 Organize information from multiple sources
5.2 Present the information
- How can I organize all the information?
- How can I present the result?

6. Evaluation

6.1 Judge the product (effectiveness)
6.2 Judge the information problem-solving program (efficiency)
- Is the task completed?
- How can I do things better?

The Big6™ Skills

The Big6 is a process model of how people of all ages solve an information problem.

1. Task Definition

1.1 Define the information problem

1.2 Identify information needed to complete the task (to solve the information problem)

- What's the task?
- What types of information do I need?

2. Information Seeking Strategies

2.1 Determine the range of possible sources (brainstorm)

2.2 Evaluate the different possible sources to determine priorities (select the best sources)

- What are possible sources?
- Which are the best?

3. Location and Access

3.1 Locate sources (intellectually and physically)

3.2 Find information within sources

- Where is each source?
- Where is the information in each source?

4. Use of Information

4.1 Engage (e.g., read, hear, view, touch) the information in a source

4.2 Extract relevant information from a source

- How can I best use each source?
- What information in each source is useful?

5. Synthesis

5.1 Organize information from multiple sources

5.2 Present the information

- How can I organize all the information?
- How can I present the result?

6. Evaluation

6.1 Judge the product (effectiveness)

6.2 Judge the information problem-solving program (efficiency)

- Is the task completed?
- How can I do things better?

The Information Age: Implications for Learning and Teaching

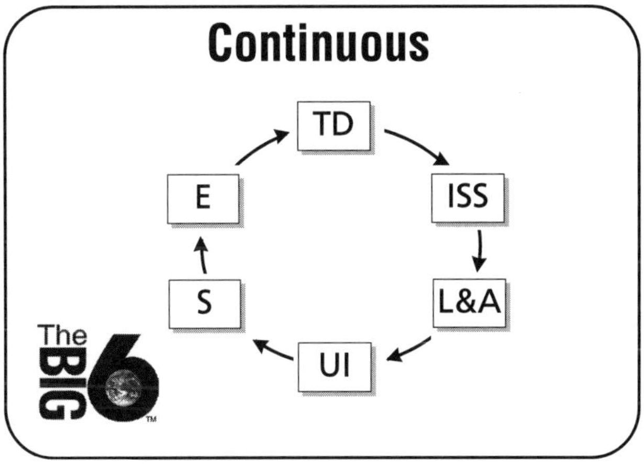

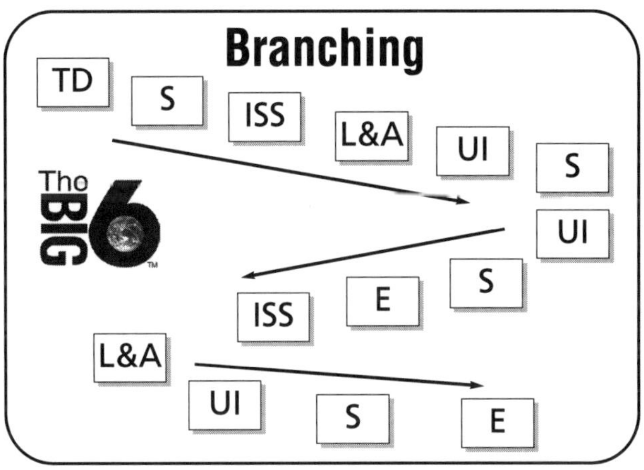

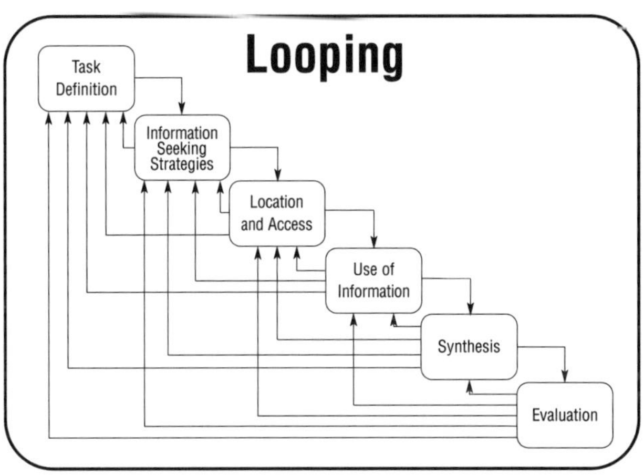

Notes:

Think Sheet

Part II: Super3

The BIG6™ Super3

Introducing the Super3: Working with the Very Youngest

by Mike Eisenberg

The Super3 contains the same basic elements as the Big6™ but makes the language and the concepts a little simpler and easier for younger students to understand. The Super3 are:

1. **Plan**—(Beginning)
2. **Do**—(Middle)
3. **Review**—(End)

This information problem-solving motto is easy to remember and fun to say, and it helps young students get a handle on information problem-solving.

Think Process!

The importance of the Super3 lies in the fact that it gets the youngest students to start thinking in terms of process. Many students are not able to see past the Do component of the process when thinking about the work that they do in school or any other information problem-solving activity. While Do is an important step in creating a product or solving a problem, it cannot exist on its own. Do works the best when it falls between Plan and Review.

To get your young students thinking in terms of process, have them imagine themselves as the main character in a story about completing the task at hand. This is a concept that every student will be able to grasp since students hear stories all the time. Now have them explain the plot line of the story; how do they prepare to tackle the assignment, problem, or task? After they describe finishing the task, have them consider whether or not this was a good story. Did the central character do a good job? Once students become comfortable with identifying the elements of the Super3, make a habit of regularly asking students to identify the Super3 steps in every story that you read together as a class. You will be surprised by how quickly they will "get" it!

Step One: Plan

Plan (Beginning) is the important first step of the Super3, and it is a step that students do not always take naturally. More often, they jump right into the middle and begin doing their assignments. The key is getting them to understand the first step's importance. When kindergarten students are given a picture to color, spend a moment with them discussing the steps that they take in choosing colors. What are they doing when they choose a blue crayon for the sky? They are planning how they will tackle the assignment to achieve the desired effect. This is really no different from a twelfth grader planning which resources he or she will consult first when writing his or her term paper about Hamlet. Helping your students begin to think in terms of process creates the foundation for educational success throughout their school careers.

Young elementary students do a great deal of planning in their daily routines. This includes:

- Choosing teams for a kickball game
- Picking blocks to use to build a castle
- Selecting a picture book to check out from the library media center
- Deciding where to place his or her mat for naptime

Planning is a natural function of human thought. It is your responsibility as an educator to help students see the importance of the planning process.

Remember to Review

Review (End) is a more difficult concept for most students to remember. Many kids feel that once they complete a task or assignment, the job is done. However, to truly build a foundation for academic success, young students must not forget to evaluate what they have produced. Just as Big6™ #6—Evaluation—asks students to evaluate both process and product, Review is a multi-faceted concept as well. When asking students about their work, do not just ask them if they created quality products. Ask them about the path that they took to complete the assignment and whether or not they would do things differently next time.

One way to get your students into the Review habit is to make it a part of your assignments. When planning an activity, build in evaluation time. Have students look over their work before they turn it in, and put their initials on the backs of their papers if they believe that what they created meets the assignment. Be very specific and clear about your expectations when assigning work to your students since this will give them a better foundation for reviewing the work that they have done.

Parents Can Help Too

Encourage parents to make evaluation a part of home life, too. Talk to parents about the importance of Review on open house night. Occasionally, send students home with a piece of paper for their parents, explaining what the students learned and did in class that day. Have parents ask their children specific questions about what they learned in class and whether or not they feel they did a good job on their assignment. This will avoid the "What did you learn at school today? Nothing" syndrome at the dinner table and will help reinforce the importance of Review outside of the classroom.

Super3 in Action

To see the Super3 in action, consider an example of an assignment given to a kindergarten class. Students are to work with a partner to draw a picture showing five winter activities. See how the Super3 could be applied. Are partners talking about which winter activities to include (Plan)? What about actually working on the project (Do)? How about looking over their pictures before they turn them in (Review)? The Super3 is super easy and will put your little ones on the road to success!

The Super3

The Super3 contains the same basic elements as the Big6 but makes the language and the concepts a little simpler and easier for younger students to understand. The Super3 are:

1. **Plan—(Beginning)**

   When students get an assignment or a task, BEFORE they start doing anything, they should think—
   - What am I supposed to do?
   - What will it look like if I do a really good job?
   - What do I need to find out to do the job?

   Big6 steps:
   - Task Definition
   - Information Seeking Strategies

2. **Do—(Middle)**

   In the middle the students DO the activity. This is where they read, view, tell, make a picture, etc.

   Big6 steps:
   - Location and Access
   - Use of Information

3. **Review—(End)**

   Before finishing the product and turning it in students should stop and think—Is this done?
   - Did I do what I was supposed to do?
   - Do I feel OK about this?
   - Should I do something else before I turn it in?

   Big6 steps:
   - Synthesis
   - Evaluation

The Super3

You are the main character in a story:

Beginning—Plan

Middle—Do

End—Review

The Super3

Sample Lessons

- **PLAN—What should it look like when I'm done? Show different examples.**
- **DO—Citing sources. Use rubber stamps.**
- **DO—Brainstorm sources. Select best.**
- **REVIEW—Show examples that are missing things.**

For the Very Young (PreK–1) The Super3

Example:

- **Making a picture of signs of spring**

Super3 Lesson

Create a "culture of citing"

Use rubber stamps

- **book**
- **computer**
- **person**
- **self**

Super3 and Costume Planning Tips (Grades K–2)

by Michelle S. Wurster, Susann L. Wurster

Your students can make decisions about their own costumes! Use this unique moment to introduce the Super3 Plan-Do-Review concepts in a real-life situation—costume planning.

The Super3 process can help students make creative decisions about what to wear for costume party fun. Use the following prompts to ask your students to think about their costume ideas:

#1 Plan—(Beginning)

- What (or who) would you like to be for a costume party?
- Make a list of choices.
- Choose your favorite character!

#2 Do—(Middle)

- Draw a picture of yourself dressed in your costume.
- Ask a grown up to help you make or buy your costume.
- Wear your costume for fun!

#3 Review—(End)

- How did your costume work out?
- Were you happy with your costume?
- Was it fun to be that character?

Rainy Day Fun with the Super3 (Grades K–2)

by Barbara A. Jansen

Think about your favorite rainy day game or activity. Use the Super3 to share it with other kids by following these directions:

1. Write a title for the activity.

   (Example: Let's Go Fishing!)

2. Write a short introduction that will make other kids want to do it.

   (Example: Hey, Kids! Do you like to fish? Here is a way to make a fishing game by using items you may find around your house and the Super3 to help!)

3. Use the Super3 to organize the instructions so any other kid can do the activity.

Plan

- In one or two sentences, tell what kids will do. Tell the main idea of the game.

  (*Example:* Make and learn to play a fishing game.)

- In one or two sentences tell kids what they need to find out about in order the make and do the activity.

  (*Example:* You need to find out what materials you need and how to make the game pieces. You need to learn the rules of the game.)

Do

- List materials that kids will need to gather. Materials that are found around the house work best.
- Write a detailed list of instructions for making the game or doing the activity.

Review

- Now instruct the kids to play the game or do the activity. Ask them questions to make sure that they have done it right. Give them some ways to change or make the activity different the next time they do it.

  (*Example:* After you play the game, think about what you liked and did not like about it. Did you follow the rules? How can you change the game to make it more interesting if you play again? Now, clean up the game pieces and put them away for another rainy day!)

4. Now, ask parents or teachers to read your rainy day activity and edit for spelling, grammar, and safety. They need to try the activity to make sure you did not leave out any steps.
5. Have your parent or teacher e-mail the activity to the Big6™ Kids Editor, Barbara Jansen at bjansen@standrews.austin.tx.us.
6. If your activity is chosen for publication on the Big6™ Kids website, we will only use your first name and last initial and your city. If you wish for us to publish your school name, please have your parent or teacher give us permission in the e-mail.

Good luck and have fun writing your rainy day activity!

Think Sheet

Part III: Learning the Big6™

Learning the Big6™

Introduction

In this part of the Workshop Handbook, we get to the heart of our approach to information and technology literacy: the Big6™. This section includes:

- Explanations of the Big6™ at different levels and for different age groups
- A chart showing the Big6™ in different contexts: school, life, and work
- Exercises that help develop a Big6™ understanding

The first set of materials explains the stages of the Big6™ as a process and as individual sets of skills. The stages are important parts of the Big6™ process. These are the necessary process stages for solving information problems and they represent a flow from beginning (figuring out what needs to be done) to middle (gathering and using necessary information) to end (creating a resulting product and evaluating success). Successful information problem-solving requires successfully completing each of these stages; however, this does not necessarily follow in a step-by-step fashion. For example, sometimes we jump from Task Definition—figuring out the scope of a project—to Synthesis—creating an outline of what the result might look like. Then, we might loop back and determine the resources we wish to use (Information Seeking Strategies) and so on. Similarly, Evaluation—determining effectiveness and efficiency—is not only an ending skill, but Evaluation occurs as students engage in every Big6™ stage. Students are constantly jumping from stages in the process to Evaluation and back.

We suggest spending some time reviewing the language of the Big6™—the formal statements describing the stages in the process, the detailed explanations for each Big6™ Skill, and the Big6™ stages as questions for elementary level children.

The Big6™ in Context

The charts that follow present the Big6™ in the context of specific settings: school, life, and work. One of the strengths of the Big6™ is its wide applicability across situations and settings. We firmly believe in making learning relevant. Students constantly question the applicability of what they learn in school. Demonstrating information's applicability is easy with the Big6™. The Big6™ Skills that children learn at school are applicable to their lives beyond school. If they become effective and efficient information problem-solvers in school, they will be effective and efficient information problem-solvers beyond school.

In addition to the chart with the three examples (an assignment for class, selecting a movie, and creating a work report), we provide a blank chart so you can brainstorm school-home-work situations from the audience. Have students work through each one according to the Big6™ in small groups or with the entire audience.

At first glance, the Big6™ often seems like common sense. "It's simple," some say—and on one level it is. However, the Big6™ also encompasses some complex critical-thinking abilities. We provide a set of worksheets to help develop Big6™ understandings and to gain an appreciation of the nuances of skills at each stage.

Big6™: Literal, Interpretive and Applied Understanding

The exercises take you through literal, interpretive, and applied levels of understanding. For example, Worksheet One requires identification of the Big6™ Skill(s) students are using when engaging in 12 different activities. This is a literal level application of the information that was previously presented. The next set of worksheets requires an interpretive response. Completing the worksheets requires application of knowledge by explaining the skills to be taught and the explanation of choices. The last group of worksheets is open-ended, providing a structure for developing more independence in order to apply understandings of the Big6™ process and skills.

We are all information consumers—in school, work, and life settings. In order to put our students in a position to be effective consumers as well, we must provide them with the tools for understanding the nature of information and using information throughout their lives. The Big6™ provides a framework for teaching them this most important lesson.

Working through this chapter increases competence in understanding the Big6™ process and the depth of thinking and skills required in each Big6™ stage.

Information Literacy: The Big6™ Skills Process and Approach

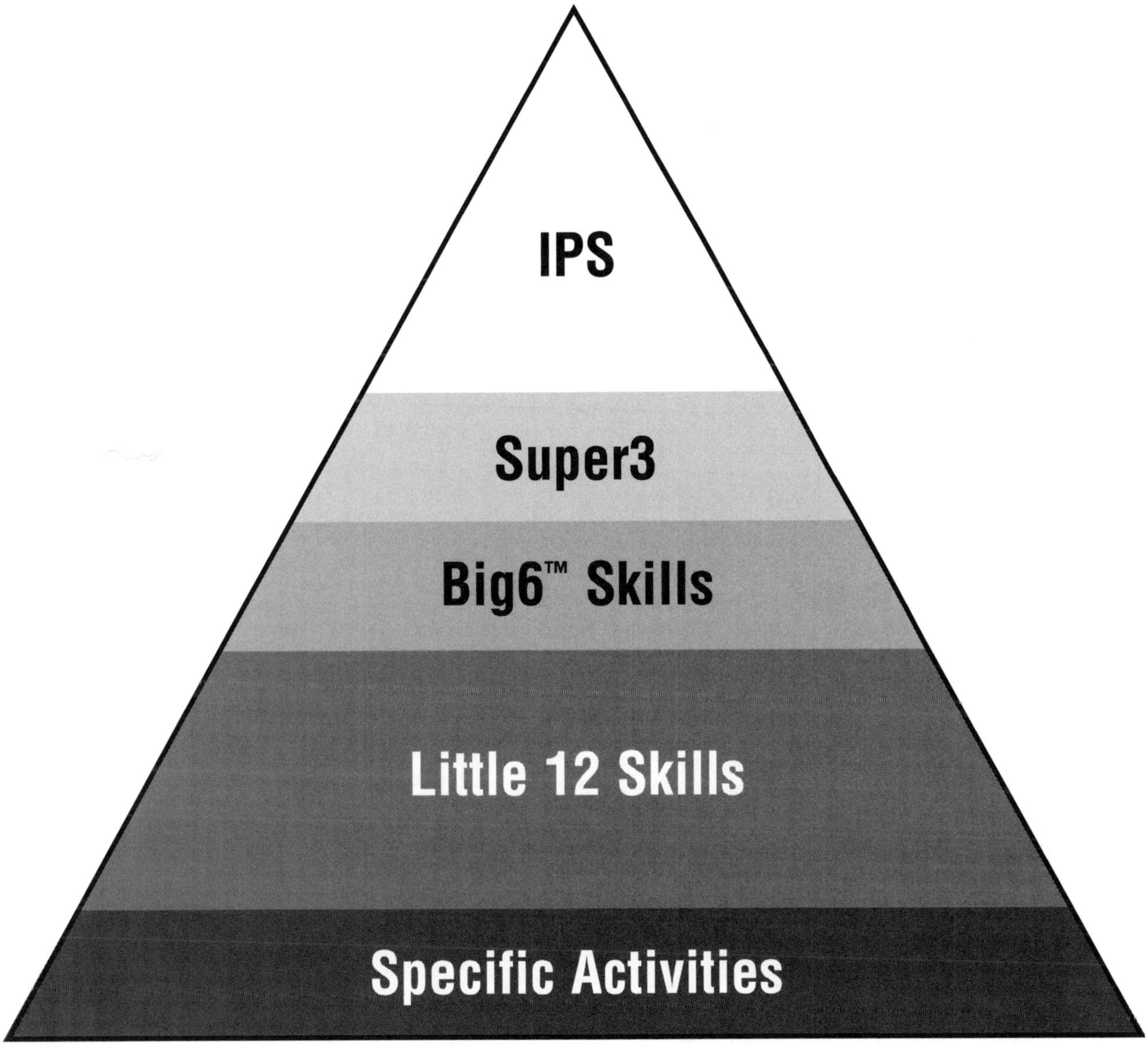

The Big6™ Skills Approach to Information Problem-Solving

1. Task Definition

1.1 Define the problem.

1.2 Identify the information needed.

2. Information Seeking Strategies

2.1 Determine all possible sources.

2.2 Select the best source.

3. Location & Access

3.1 Locate sources.

3.2 Find information within sources.

4. Use of Information

4.1 Engage (e.g., read, hear, view).

4.2 Extract relevant information.

5. Synthesis

5.1 Organize information from multiple sources.

5.2 Present the result.

6. Evaluation

6.1 Judge the result (effectiveness).

6.2 Judge the process (efficiency).

Big6™ #1
Task Definition

The student demonstrates the ability to:

- Determine the information problem to be solved
- Reformulate a complete statement of the task
- Pick out keywords embedded in a question
- Ask a good question
- Understand and follow printed and/or oral directions

Big6™ #2
Information Seeking Strategies

The student demonstrates the ability to:

- Develop alternatives and to seek a variety of materials
- Determine which information is most/least important
- Recognize that information can be gathered from many sources, including investigation, observation, and human resources
- Use appropriate criteria for selecting sources

Big6™ #3
Location and Access

The student demonstrates the ability to:

- Determine what sources are available
- Independently gather resources
- Determine if the source is usable
- Access appropriate information systems, including online databases, online public access catalog, and electronic multimedia

Big6™ #4
Use of Information

The student demonstrates the ability to:

- Distinguish facts from opinion
- Accurately and completely summarize/paraphrase the main idea from written and oral sources
- Accurately cite sources
- Read, listen, view, and touch carefully to acquire information

Big6™ #5
Synthesis

The student demonstrates the ability to:

- Organize information in clear, coherent presentations
- Present information in ways appropriate to the task
- Participate effectively in discussions and debates
- Produce personally designed products to communicate content

Big6™ #6
Evaluation

The student demonstrates the ability to:

- Demonstrate a high degree of confidence in the quality of the product produced
- Assess the product for completeness, strengths, and weaknesses
- Develop criteria to determine the effectiveness of the process used to solve the problem
- Provide recommendations to improve results
- Determine the need for further information

Information Problem-Solving in School, Life, and Work Contexts

Information Problem-Solving Process	School Context: Completing an assignment for class	Life Context: Deciding which movie to attend on Saturday night	Work Context: Reporting on five year product sales
Task Definition	Finding out that the task involves writing a two-part essay and realizing that a key to success is using documented supporting evidence.	Figuring out that it will be necessary to attend a 7:00–7:30 p.m. showing in order to get the babysitter home on time.	Producing a readable chart representing sales figures by product and salesperson. Determining that reliable sales data by department will be needed.
Information Seeking Strategies	Considering all potential information sources and deciding that current journals and newspapers would be best.	Deciding to look at the entertainment section of the newspaper to determine the showing times of movies.	Determining that there are two places where sales figures are kept: on paper and on computer disks. Deciding to use the computer version.
Location & Access	Using an online index to search for appropriate periodical articles. Finding the articles online and in print.	Locating the newspaper upstairs next to the bed. Using the "Quick Guide" on the first page to locate the entertainment section.	Finding disks with the sales data and identifying the relevant files.
Use of Information	Reading the articles and typing notes directly into a word processing program, noting the sources.	Reading the movie ads and focusing on times and locations.	Examining the various files, then cutting and pasting the data by relevant categories and years.
Synthesis	Using a word processor, creating an outline, then drafting the essay.	Determining that there is only one movie playing at the time you both want to see a movie.	Using an electronic spreadsheet program to combine the various sales data and generating a chart from the spreadsheet.
Evaluation	Realizing that your details are weak on one of the two parts and that you need to go back and find additional information.	Realizing that the newspaper was a good source for the necessary information and that you successfully met your task.	Being congratulated by your manager for a nice job; recognizing that the spreadsheet software was more than adequate for the task.

Worksheet 3-1—Information Problem-Solving in School, Life, and Work Contexts

Information Problem-Solving Process	School Context	Life Context	Work Context
Task Definition			
Information Seeking Strategies			
Location & Access			
Use of Information			
Synthesis			
Evaluation			

Developing Big6™ Understandings

Worksheet 3-2—Literal Level: Identify the Big6™

In the space provided, indicate which of the Big6™ Skills students are using when they perform each of the following activities:

TD	=	Task Definition
ISS	=	Information Seeking Strategies
L&A	=	Location & Access
UI	=	Use of Information
S	=	Synthesis
E	=	Evaluation

When a student:

______ 1. chooses between an encyclopedia and a magazine for information on the political situation in the Middle East.

______ 2. creates a weekly classroom newsletter about freedom movements in the world.

______ 3. interviews a long-time community resident about local history.

______ 4. assesses the presentations of other students.

______ 5. uses *PowerPoint* to create a multimedia show about holiday celebrations in other cultures.

______ 6. reflects on personal information skills that need improving.

______ 7. uses appropriate Yahoo or Alta Vista commands.

______ 8. evaluates the effectiveness of different specific media (e.g. political ads, car commercials, video vs. audio, etc.).

______ 9. writes a thesis statement.

______ 10. finds word definitions in a dictionary.

______ 11. answers questions using a textbook.

______ 12. selects a specific topic for a science fair project.

See Answer Key p.52

Worksheet 3-3—Interpretive Level: Science Homework

Curriculum Context: For homework, Sally must answer questions at the end of a chapter in her science textbook.

Student Activities	Big6™	Explanation
Sally decides that she will need to use her science book to answer the questions.		
Sally writes the answers to the questions, noting the page number(s) where she found the answers.		
Sally thinks about how she used the bold headings to locate the answers and realizes it was a helpful technique.		
Sally calls her friend Tanya about the assignment. Tanya reminds Sally to write the answers in complete sentences.		
Sally reads a section looking for the answer to question four.		
Sally uses the bold headings to get the section that seems to be the right one for question four.		

Big6™ Skills

1. **Task Definition**
   1.1 Define the problem.
   1.2 Identify the information needed.
2. **Information Seeking Strategies**
   2.1 Determine all possible sources.
   2.2 Select the best source.
3. **Location & Access**
   3.1 Locate sources.
   3.2 Find information within sources.
4. **Use of Information**
   4.1 Engage (e.g., read, hear, view).
   4.2 Extract relevant information.
5. **Synthesis**
   5.1 Organize information from multiple sources.
   5.2 Present the result.
6. **Evaluation**
   6.1 Judge the result (effectiveness).
   6.2 Judge the process (efficiency).

See Answer Key p.52

Worksheet 3-4—Interpretive Level: Social Studies

Curriculum Context: Middle school students are working on interdisciplinary group projects on regions of the United States, including cultural, social, geographic, and historical aspects.

Student Activities	Big6™	Explanation
Group three uses the online catalog to find books while group four is using the periodical index.		
The groups brainstorm possible sources of information and decide to use magazines, books, their parents, and the World Wide Web.		
The students discuss which Web sites were useful and why.		
Group four prints out a magazine article.		
Each student group selects an area of the United States as the focus of its report.		
Group five delivers its report in the form of a TV news show.		

The Big6™ Skills © 1987 Eisenberg & Berkowitz

Big6™ Skills

1. **Task Definition**
   - 1.1 Define the problem.
   - 1.2 Identify the information needed.
2. **Information Seeking Strategies**
   - 2.1 Determine all possible sources.
   - 2.2 Select the best source.
3. **Location & Access**
   - 3.1 Locate sources.
   - 3.2 Find information within sources.
4. **Use of Information**
   - 4.1 Engage (e.g., read, hear, view).
   - 4.2 Extract relevant information.
5. **Synthesis**
   - 5.1 Organize information from multiple sources.
   - 5.2 Present the result.
6. **Evaluation**
   - 6.1 Judge the result (effectiveness).
   - 6.2 Judge the process (efficiency).

See Answer Key p.52

Worksheet 3-5—Interpretive Level: Literature Essay

Curriculum Context: Joe, a 10th grade student, has just finished reading *The Call of the Wild.* As part of a take-home exam, he is required to write an essay comparing various aspects of his life to Buck's life.

Student Activities	Big6™	Explanation
Joe marks appropriate sections in the book with paper clips then enters some relevant quotations in a word processing document.		
Joe realizes that he earned an A on his essay because he referred to specific examples in the book.		
Joe scans through the book to find the section where Buck first hears the "call of the wild."		
Joe realizes that the task involves writing a coherent and organized essay with specific comparisons between his life and Buck's life.		
Joe determines that it will be necessary to use a copy of *The Call of the Wild*, but a critical analysis would also help.		
Joe prepares a chart of events in his life and in Buck's life, then uses word processing to write and print his essay.		

Big6™ Skills

1. **Task Definition**
   1.1 Define the problem.
   1.2 Identify the information needed.
2. **Information Seeking Strategies**
   2.1 Determine all possible sources.
   2.2 Select the best source.
3. **Location & Access**
   3.1 Locate sources.
   3.2 Find information within sources.
4. **Use of Information**
   4.1 Engage (e.g., read, hear, view).
   4.2 Extract relevant information.
5. **Synthesis**
   5.1 Organize information from multiple sources.
   5.2 Present the result.
6. **Evaluation**
   6.1 Judge the result (effectiveness).
   6.2 Judge the process (efficiency).

See Answer Key p.52

Worksheet 3-6—Interpretive Level: Animals Picture Book

Curriculum Context: A 2nd grade class is studying animals that live in a nearby area. Each student is to make a book that includes a picture of three animals and a very short story (a sentence or two) about each animal.

Student Activities	Big6™	Explanation
The students and teacher brainstorm to identify some animals that live in a nearby area. Students may use one from this list but must decide on two others on their own.		
The teacher debriefs with the class. What was the most difficult part of the assignment?		
The library media specialist helps the students find the books and magazines about animals in the library media center.		
The students decide that a visit to a local nature center would be helpful.		
The library media specialist shows students how to write notes about their animals on index cards.		
Some students draw pictures of the animals with crayons or paint while other students paste pictures from old magazines.		

Big6™ Skills

1. **Task Definition**
   1.1 Define the problem.
   1.2 Identify the information needed.
2. **Information Seeking Strategies**
   2.1 Determine all possible sources.
   2.2 Select the best source.
3. **Location & Access**
   3.1 Locate sources.
   3.2 Find information within sources.
4. **Use of Information**
   4.1 Engage (e.g., read, hear, view).
   4.2 Extract relevant information.
5. **Synthesis**
   5.1 Organize information from multiple sources.
   5.2 Present the result.
6. **Evaluation**
   6.1 Judge the result (effectiveness).
   6.2 Judge the process (efficiency).

See Answer Key p.52

Worksheet 3-7—Interpretive Level: Family History Chart

Curriculum Context: Students in a 4th grade class are studying their family histories. Each student is to construct a chart listing one significant family event and one significant U.S. historical event for each year of his or her life.

Student Activities	Big6™	Explanation
Students decide that some possible sources for U.S. history information are: their textbooks, the CD-ROM references, and possibly the World Wide Web.		
After trying to draw a chart by hand, a student uses a graphing program to construct the chart of his or her family events and U.S. historical events.		
A student uses a microcassette recorder to tape an interview with his or her parents about the important events in the student's life.		
By comparing charts with each other, the students decide they could prepare neater and more legible charts if they learned how to use computers.		
Students determine that the task will require them to use both personal and U.S. history information.		
A student uses Google to search for U.S. history information on the World Wide Web.		

Big6™ Skills

1. **Task Definition**
   1.1 Define the problem.
   1.2 Identify the information needed.
2. **Information Seeking Strategies**
   2.1 Determine all possible sources.
   2.2 Select the best source.
3. **Location & Access**
   3.1 Locate sources.
   3.2 Find information within sources.
4. **Use of Information**
   4.1 Engage (e.g., read, hear, view).
   4.2 Extract relevant information.
5. **Synthesis**
   5.1 Organize information from multiple sources.
   5.2 Present the result.
6. **Evaluation**
   6.1 Judge the result (effectiveness).
   6.2 Judge the process (efficiency).

See Answer Key p.52

Worksheet 3-8—Interpretive Level: Vocabulary Homework

Curriculum Context: Students in 9th grade are given a vocabulary list of literary devices (e.g., metaphor, allusion, hyperbole, etc.) to define. The teacher requires that they rewrite the definitions in their own words and provide an example of each device.

Student Activities	Big6™	Explanation
Students use the glossary in the back of the book to find a term.		
The teacher says that students can use a dictionary or the glossary in the textbook.		
Each student assesses the amount of time that the assignment took.		
Students determine that to be successful they must write the definitions in their own words.		
Students make a word processed list of terms and rewritten definitions.		
A student takes notes from the dictionary before writing the definition in his or her own words.		

The Big6™ Skills © 1987 Eisenberg & Berkowitz

Big6™ Skills

1. **Task Definition**
   1.1 Define the problem.
   1.2 Identify the information needed.
2. **Information Seeking Strategies**
   2.1 Determine all possible sources.
   2.2 Select the best source.
3. **Location & Access**
   3.1 Locate sources.
   3.2 Find information within sources.
4. **Use of Information**
   4.1 Engage (e.g., read, hear, view).
   4.2 Extract relevant information.
5. **Synthesis**
   5.1 Organize information from multiple sources.
   5.2 Present the result.
6. **Evaluation**
   6.1 Judge the result (effectiveness).
   6.2 Judge the process (efficiency).

See Answer Key p.52

Worksheet 3-9—Interpretive Level: Music Note and Rest Values

Curriculum Context: Students in a 4th grade music class are studying "note and rest values."

Student Activities	Big6™	Explanation
One group creates a computer quiz in *PowerPoint.*		
The class discusses which of the tests were hard and why.		
The teacher explains that students will be working in groups and the assignment is to make a test for others.		
The library media specialist leads the students to the music books.		
One group decides that it wants some more information and heads to the library media center.		
Students photocopy pages from three books in the library media center.		

Big6™ Skills

1. **Task Definition**
   - 1.1 Define the problem.
   - 1.2 Identify the information needed.
2. **Information Seeking Strategies**
   - 2.1 Determine all possible sources.
   - 2.2 Select the best source.
3. **Location & Access**
   - 3.1 Locate sources.
   - 3.2 Find information within sources.
4. **Use of Information**
   - 4.1 Engage (e.g., read, hear, view).
   - 4.2 Extract relevant information.
5. **Synthesis**
   - 5.1 Organize information from multiple sources.
   - 5.2 Present the result.
6. **Evaluation**
   - 6.1 Judge the result (effectiveness).
   - 6.2 Judge the process (efficiency).

See Answer Key p.52

Worksheet 3-10—Applied Level: Nutrition Posters

Describe one or two activities that relate to each of the Big6™ Skills for the following curriculum content.

Curriculum Context: Students in a 1st grade class are studying nutrition and food groups. Students are required to make posters that describe what they learned. Each poster should include examples of foods that belong in each food group. Additionally, each food group must be correctly labeled.

Big6™	Student Activities

The Big6™ Skills © 1987 Eisenberg & Berkowitz

Big6™ Skills

1. **Task Definition**
   1.1 Define the problem.
   1.2 Identify the information needed.
2. **Information Seeking Strategies**
   2.1 Determine all possible sources.
   2.2 Select the best source.
3. **Location & Access**
   3.1 Locate sources.
   3.2 Find information within sources.
4. **Use of Information**
   4.1 Engage (e.g., read, hear, view).
   4.2 Extract relevant information.
5. **Synthesis**
   5.1 Organize information from multiple sources.
   5.2 Present the result.
6. **Evaluation**
   6.1 Judge the result (effectiveness).
   6.2 Judge the process (efficiency).

Worksheet 3-11—Applied Level: Earth Science Project

Describe one or two activities that relate to each of the Big6™ Skills for the following curriculum content.

Curriculum Context: A 7th grade science class is studying rocks. Students are required to demonstrate their knowledge by preparing a special project that shows what they learned about the types of rocks and how they were formed.

Big6™	Student Activities

The Big6™ Skills © 1987 Eisenberg & Berkowitz

Big6™ Skills

1. **Task Definition**
   1.1 Define the problem.
   1.2 Identify the information needed.
2. **Information Seeking Strategies**
   2.1 Determine all possible sources.
   2.2 Select the best source.
3. **Location & Access**
   3.1 Locate sources.
   3.2 Find information within sources.
4. **Use of Information**
   4.1 Engage (e.g., read, hear, view).
   4.2 Extract relevant information.
5. **Synthesis**
   5.1 Organize information from multiple sources.
   5.2 Present the result.
6. **Evaluation**
   6.1 Judge the result (effectiveness).
   6.2 Judge the process (efficiency).

Worksheet 3-12—Applied Level: Social Studies Group Report

Describe one or two activities that relate to each of the Big6™ Skills for the following curriculum content.

Curriculum Context: Students in an 11th grade class are divided into small groups to study significant Supreme Court cases. Each group is assigned a specific case on which to report. Next, each group is required to prepare a three-part project (oral, visual, and written products) to explain the background, the decision, and the impact of the decision. When they are finished, each group will share its research with the rest of the class.

Big6™	Student Activities

The Big6™ Skills © 1987 Eisenberg & Berkowitz

Big6™ Skills

1. **Task Definition**
   1.1 Define the problem.
   1.2 Identify the information needed.
2. **Information Seeking Strategies**
   2.1 Determine all possible sources.
   2.2 Select the best source.
3. **Location & Access**
   3.1 Locate sources.
   3.2 Find information within sources.
4. **Use of Information**
   4.1 Engage (e.g., read, hear, view).
   4.2 Extract relevant information.
5. **Synthesis**
   5.1 Organize information from multiple sources.
   5.2 Present the result.
6. **Evaluation**
   6.1 Judge the result (effectiveness).
   6.2 Judge the process (efficiency).

Worksheet 3-13 —Integrated Curriculum Situation

Create a typical, integrated curriculum situation. Describe one or two activities that relate to each of the Big6™ Skills.

Curriculum Context:

Big6™ Skills	Activities
1. Task Definition 1.1 Define the problem. 1.2 Identify the information needed.	
2. Information Seeking Strategies 2.1 Determine all possible sources. 2.2 Select the best source.	
3. Location & Access 3.1 Locate sources. 3.2 Find information within sources.	
4. Use of Information 4.1 Engage (e.g., read, hear, view). 4.2 Extract relevant information.	
5. Synthesis 5.1 Organize information from multiple sources. 5.2 Present the result.	
6. Evaluation 6.1 Judge the result (effectiveness). 6.2 Judge the process (efficiency).	

Worksheet 3-13—(continued)

Create a typical, integrated curriculum situation. Describe one or two activities that relate to each of the Big6™ Skills.

Curriculum Context:

Big6™ Skills	Activities
1. Task Definition 1.1 Define the problem. 1.2 Identify the information needed.	
2. Information Seeking Strategies 2.1 Determine all possible sources. 2.2 Select the best source.	
3. Location & Access 3.1 Locate sources. 3.2 Find information within sources.	
4. Use of Information 4.1 Engage (e.g., read, hear, view). 4.2 Extract relevant information.	
5. Synthesis 5.1 Organize information from multiple sources. 5.2 Present the result.	
6. Evaluation 6.1 Judge the result (effectiveness). 6.2 Judge the process (efficiency).	

Worksheet 3-14

Curriculum Standards	Big6™ Connection

Answer Key, pages 38–45 (for Part III)

3-2
ISS
S
UI
E
S
E
L&A
E
TD or S
L&A
UI
TD

3-3
ISS
S
E
TD
UI
L&A

3-4
L&A
ISS
E
UI
TD
S

3-5
UI
E
L&A
TD
ISS
S

3-6
TD
E
L&A
ISS
UI
S

3-7
ISS
S
UI
E
TD
L&A

3-8
L&A
ISS
E
TD
S
UI

3-9
S
E
TD
ISS
L&A
UI

Part IV: Technology and the Big6™

Technology and the Big6™

Introduction

Technology and technology skills are integral to the Big6™ process and approach. K–12 schools are finally moving away from teaching computer skills in isolation, as skills to be applied at a later time or in lab settings separate from the classroom. Students need to be able to use computers flexibly, creatively, and purposefully. Today, educators at all levels are seeking to move from teaching isolated computer skills to teaching integrated information and technology skills.

For us, that means integrating computer skills within the Big6™ problem-solving process. Individual computer skills take on a new meaning when they are integrated within the Big6™, and students develop true "computer literacy" because they have genuinely applied various computer and technology skills as part of the learning process. Considering technology within a Big6™ context provides the necessary structure and framework for this to happen. Effective integration of information and technology skills learning has two requirements: (1) the skills must directly relate to the content area curriculum and to classroom assignments and (2) the skills themselves need to be tied together in a logical and systematic information process model. The same trend is taking place in relation to teaching computer skills.

Big6™ and Technology in Context

The first page in this section sets the technology context. The *PowerPoint* handout in this section displays the slides that Mike uses to present his thoughts on the current and immediate future state of technology. As noted in the introduction to Part I, we expect you to supplement these *PowerPoint* slides with slides of your own.

The next two worksheets are used in an exercise to demonstrate the relationship between technology and the Big6. Technology skills are easily integrated into the Big6™ Skills model. The first column—Baseline Technologies—is used for non-electronic tools that students use. A crayon with paper, for example, is a baseline technology that can be entered into the top line in the first column. Now, what's the related Big6™ Skill(s)? Where in the Big6™ does a crayon with paper prove valuable? The answer is Synthesis, and that can be entered into the second column. Finally, what are the related electronic technologies that provide a similar boost to crayon and paper, only more so? The answer should include software such as paint or draw, graphics programs, or even video editing. These can be entered into the third column.

Baseline Technologies	Related Big6™ Skills	Related Electronic Technologies
■ The yellow pages	■ Location & Access	■ Search tools/engines; indexes
■ A highlighter	■ Use of Information	■ Copy and paste
■ Books and magazines	■ Information Seeking Strategies	■ Full-text electronic resources
■ A pen and paper	■ Use of Information/Synthesis	■ Word processing; desktop publishing; presentation software
■ The telephone	■ Location & Access	■ E-mail
■ A face-to-face meeting	■ Task Definition/Information Seeking Strategies, Location & Access, Use of Information, Synthesis, and Evaluation	■ E-mail, chat, audio or video conferencing

After the exercise, the relationship can be turned around using the next worksheet. That is, for each of the Big6™ stages indicate the related electronic technologies. This chart forms the basis of the Big6™-technology connection. For example, word processing, desktop publishing, *PowerPoint*, and other presentation software programs are used for Synthesis (to organize and present). Word processing is also important for Use of Information (note-taking). Online databases, CD-ROM encyclopedias, and other electronic resources are part of an effective Information Seeking Strategy and provide Location & Access capabilities. Various Internet capabilities are also included in information problem-solving. E-mail is highly useful for linking students with their teachers or each other for Task Definition activities and later for Evaluation. Web browsers and search engines (e.g., Yahoo, Google, AltaVista) are used in Information Seeking Strategies and as tools for location and access. FTP and downloading/uploading help students to use information. When integrated into the information problem-solving process, these technological capabilities become powerful information tools for students.

The Big6™-technology connection is further explained in the "Technology Within the Big6™ Framework" chart and the reprinted ERIC Digest. The final chart, "Information Services—Including Technology," links various library media services to various technologies.

Technology: Today and Tomorrow

Technology—Out of Context

Word processing Electronic spreadsheets
E-mail Web browsing Spell/grammar check
Web page design
Telnet Instant messaging Chat
Statistical analysis presentation
Multimedia presentation (PowerPoint) Web searching
Online catalogs Video production
Inspiration Database management systems
Graphics CAD/CAM Group discussion Electronic indexes
Use of operating systems ftp Copy/paste
HTML Brainstorming software
Algorithms Programming PDAs

Better, But Still Out of Context

- E-mail
- Word processing
- Group discussion
- Online catalogs
- Electronic indexes
- Web browsing
- Web searching
- Electronic spreadsheets
- Upload/download
- HTML
- Spell/grammar check
- Brainstorming software
- PDAs
- Video production
- Algorithms
- Multimedia production (PowerPoint, Hyperstudio)
- ftp
- Chat
- Graphics
- Inspiration
- Database management
- Use of operating systems
- Web page design
- Copy/paste
- Statistical analysis presentation CAD/CAM
- Telnet
- Programming
- Instant messaging

Technology in Context

TASK DEFINITION	Students use e-mail, listservs, newsgroups, chat, videoconferencing, and other online communication methods to clarify assignments and brainstorm problems. May also use software to generate timelines, organizational charts, etc. to plan and organize complex problems.
INFO SEEKING STRATEGIES	Students identify and assess computerized resources as they develop information seeking strategies toward their problem.
LOCATION & ACCESS	Students use online catalogs, searchable periodical indexes, electronic encyclopedias, Web search engines, and other online searching tools to locate useful information.
USE OF INFORMATION	Students connect to and access online or locally stored electronic information sources, view, download, and decompress files, and use copy-and-paste features to extract relevant information.
SYNTHESIS	Students organize and communicate their results using word processing, database management, spreadsheet and graphics software, and distribute their projects via e-mail, Web publishing, or other media.
EVALUATION	Students evaluate the impact of the technology they used, including its effectiveness and efficiency. Students use e-mail, mailing lists, newsgroups, chat, videoconferencing, and other online communication methods to gain feedback from teachers.

Notes:

Worksheet 4-1—Technology Within the Big6™ Framework

Baseline Technology	Related Big6™ Skill(s)	Related Electronic Technologies

Worksheet 4-2—Technology Within the Big6™ Framework

Use	Technology	Notes
1. Task Definition 1.1 Define the problem. 1.2 Identify the information needed.		
2. Information Seeking Strategies 2.1 Determine all possible sources. 2.2 Select the best source.		
3. Location & Access 3.1 Locate sources. 3.2 Find information within sources.		
4. Use of Information 4.1 Engage (e.g., read, hear, view). 4.2 Extract relevant information.		
5. Synthesis 5.1 Organizc information from multiple sources. 5.2 Present the result.		
6. Evaluation 6.1 Judge the result (effectiveness). 6.2 Judge the process (efficiency).		

Technology Within the Big6™ Framework

Task Definition	Students use e-mail, listservs, newsgroups, chat, videoconferencing, and other online communication methods to clarify assignments and brainstorm problems. May also use software to generate timelines, organizational charts, etc. to plan and organize complex problems.
Info Seeking Strategies	Students identify and assess computerized resources as they develop information seeking strategies toward their problem.
Location & Access	Students use online catalogs, searchable periodical indexes, electronic encyclopedias, Web search engines, and other online searching tools to locate useful information.
Use of Information	Students connect to and access online or locally stored electronic information sources, view, download, and decompress files, and use copy-and-paste features to extract relevant information.
Synthesis	Students organize and communicate their results using word processing, database management, spreadsheet and graphics software, and distribute their projects via e-mail, Web publishing, or other media.
Evaluation	Students evaluate the impact of the technology they used, including its effectiveness and efficiency. Students use e-mail, mailing lists, newsgroups, chat, videoconferencing, and other online communication methods to gain feedback from teachers.

Resources for the Big6™ and Technology

1. Task Definition

Topic a http://www.topic a.com
Yahoo Groups http://groups.yahoo.com
Andy Carvin's Ed List http://www.edwebproject.org/lists.html

2. Information Seeking Strategies

Graphic Organizers http://www.graphic.org/concept.html
Inspiration http://www.inspiration.com/
MindManager http://www.mindjet.com/index.html

3. Location and Access

Search Engine Watch http://searchenginewatch.com/
Choosing a Search Engine http://library.albany.edu/internet/choose.html
Google http://www.google.com
Vivisimo http://www.vivisimo.com
Maximizing Google http://webquest.sdsu.edu/searching/fournets.htm
Yahoo http://www.yahoo.com
Ask Jeeves http://www.askjeeves.com
Invisible Web http://www.invisibleweb.com/
Uncovering the Hidden Web http://www.ericit.org/digests/EDO-IR-2001-02.shtml
Internet Detective http://www.netskills.ac.uk/TonicNG/cgi/sesame?detective

4. Use of Information

Citations - http://oslis.k12.or.us/citeintro/citeintro.php?Grd=Elem
http://www.landmark-project.com/citation machine/cm.php
http://wizard.imsa.edu/cite
Copyright in K-12 http://www.kcsd.k12.pa.us/technology/copyright/index.html
QUality Information ChecKlist http://www.quick.org.uk/menu.htm
Hoaxes & Urban Legends http://www.snopes.com
U.S. DOE CIAC http://ciac.llnl.gov/ciac/CIACHome.html
Are They Real? http://chaucer.unh.edu/real.html
e-literate video http://newliteracies.gseis.ucla.edu/video/index.html

5. Synthesis

Organizing Information http://ipl.si.umich.edu/div/teen/aplus/linksorganizing.htm
http://feteens.com/HomeworkTestHelp/HowToFindStuff/OrganizeInfo.html
3DWriting & 3DWriter http://www.3dwriting.com
Plagiarism http://www.srsd.org/search/studentprojects/2002/plagiarism/main.html
http://newark.rutgers.edu/~ehrlich/plagiarism598.html
http://www.plagiarism.org/
http://www.utoronto.ca/writing/plagsep.html

6. Evaluation

Rubistar http://rubistar.4teachers.org
Rubrics from the Staff Room http://www.quadro.net/~ecoxon/Reporting/rubrics.htm

Prepared by Art Wolinsky, awolinsky@3dwriting.com
All links active as of 8/5/03

ERIC

ERIC Digest

ERIC Clearinghouse on Information & Technology at Syracuse University
621 Skytop Road, Suite 160
Syracuse, New York 13244
www.ericit.org
EDO-IR-2002-04

September 2002

EDO-IR-2002-04

Learning and Teaching Information Technology

Computer Skills in Context

By Michael B. Eisenberg and Doug Johnson

There is clear and widespread agreement among the public and educators that all students need to be proficient computer users or "computer literate." However, while districts are spending a great deal of money on technology, there seems to be only a vague notion of what computer literacy really means. Can the student who operates a computer well enough to play a game, send e-mail or surf the Web be considered computer literate? Will a student who uses computers in school only for running tutorials or an integrated learning system have the skills necessary to survive in our society? Will the ability to do basic word processing be sufficient for students entering the workplace or post-secondary education?

Clearly not. In too many schools, teachers and students still use computers only as the equivalent of expensive flash cards, electronic worksheets, or as little more than a typewriter. The productivity side of computer use in the general content area curriculum is neglected or grossly underdeveloped (Moursund, 1995).

Recent publications by educational associations are advocating for a more meaningful use of technology in schools (ISTE, 2000). Educational technologists are clearly describing what students should know and be able to do with technology. They are advocating integrating computer skills into the content areas, proclaiming that computer skills should not be taught in isolation and that separate "computer classes" do not really help students learn to apply computer skills in meaningful ways. There is increasing recognition that the end result of computer literacy is not knowing how to operate computers, but to use technology as a tool for organization, communication, research, and problem solving. This is an important shift in approach and emphasis.

Moving from teaching isolated technology skills to an integrated approach is an important step that takes a great deal of planning and effort. Fortunately, we have a model for doing so. Over the past 25 years, library media professionals have worked hard to move from teaching isolated "library skills" to teaching integrated "information skills." They found that information skills can be integrated effectively when the skills (1) directly relate to the content area curriculum and to classroom assignments, and (2) are tied together in a logical and systematic information process model.

Schools seeking to move from isolated information technology skills instruction will also need to focus on both of these requirements. Successful integrated information skills programs are designed around collaborative projects jointly planned and taught by teachers and library media professionals. Information technology skills instruction can and should be imbedded in such a curriculum. Library media specialists, computer teachers, and classroom teachers need to work together to develop units and lessons that will include both technology skills, information skills, and content-area curriculum outcomes.

A meaningful, unified information technology literacy curriculum must be more than a "laundry list" of isolated skills, such as knowing the parts of the computer, writing drafts and final products with a word processor, and searching for information using the World Wide Web.

While these specific skills are important for students to learn, the "laundry list" approach does not provide an adequate model for students to transfer and apply skills from situation to situation. These curricula address the "how" of computer use, but rarely the "when" or "why." Students may learn isolated skills and tools, but they would still lack an understanding of how those various skills fit together to solve problems and complete tasks. Students need to be able to use computers and other technologies flexibly, creatively and purposefully. All learners should be able to recognize what they need to accomplish, determine whether a computer will help them to do so, and then be able to use the computer as part of the process of accomplishing their task. Individual computer skills take on a new meaning when they are integrated within this type of information problem-solving process, and students develop true "information technology literacy" because they have genuinely applied various information technology skills as part of the learning process.

The curriculum outlined on pages 2-3 of this ERIC Digest, "Technology Skills for Information Problem Solving," demonstrates how technology literacy skills can fit within an information literacy skills context (American Association of School Librarians, 1998). The baseline information literacy context is the Big6™ process (see sidebar and Eisenberg & Berkowitz, 1988, 1992, 1999, 2000). The various technology skills are adapted from the International Society for Technology in Education's National Educational Technology Standards for Students (2000) and the Mankato Schools Information Literacy Curriculum Guideline. Students might reasonably be expected to authentically demonstrate these basic computer skills before graduation.

Some technology literacy competencies that may be relevant in some situations include: (1) knowing the basic operation, terminology, and maintenance of equipment, (2) knowing how to use computer-assisted instructional programs, (3) having knowledge of the impact of technology on careers, society, and culture (as a direct instructional objective), and (4) computer programming.

Defining and describing technology skills is only a first step in assuring all our children become proficient information and technology users. A teacher-supported scope and sequence of skills, well designed projects, and effective assessments are also critical. Equally essential is collaboration among classroom teachers, teacher librarians, and technology teachers in order to present students with a unified and integrated approach to ensure that all children master the skills they will need to thrive in an information rich future (Eisenberg & Lowe, 1999).

Technology Skills for Information Problem Solving

A Curriculum Based on the Big6 Skills Approach

© Michael B. Eisenberg, Doug Johnson and Robert E. Berkowitz

Permission is granted for educational use or reprint of all or parts of this curriculum as long as the authors are properly and prominently credited.

1. Task Definition

The first part in the information problem-solving process involves recognizing that an information need exists, defining the problem, and identifying the types and amount of information needed. In terms of technology, students will be able to:

A. Communicate with teachers regarding assignments, tasks, and information problems using e-mail; online discussions (e.g., listservs, threaded Web-based discussions, newsgroups); real-time communications (e.g., instant messaging services, chat rooms, IP telephony); desktop teleconferencing; and groupware on the Internet, intranets, and local area networks.

B. Generate topics, define problems, and facilitate cooperative activities among groups of students locally and globally using e-mail, online discussions, real-time communications, desktop teleconferencing, and groupware on the Internet and local area networks.

C. Generate topics, define problems, and facilitate cooperative activities with subject area experts locally and globally using e-mail, online discussions, real-time communications, desktop teleconferencing, and groupware on the Internet and local area networks.

D. Define or refine the information problem using computerized graphic organization, brainstorming or idea generating software. This includes developing a research question or perspective on a topic.

2. Information Seeking Strategies

Once the information problem has been formulated, the student must consider all possible information sources and develop a plan for searching. Students will be able to:

A. Assess the value of various types of electronic resources for data gathering, including databases, CD-ROM resources, commercial and Internet online resources, electronic reference works, community and government information electronic resources.

B. Assess the need for and value of primary resources including interviews, surveys, experiments, and documents that are accessible through electronic means.

C. Identify and apply specific criteria for evaluating computerized electronic resources.

D. Identify and apply specific criteria for constructing meaningful original data gathering tools such as online surveys, electronic interviews, or scientific data gathering tools such as probes, meters, and timers.

E. Assess the value of e-mail, online discussions, real-time communications, desktop teleconferencing, and groupware on the Internet and local area networks as part of a search of the current literature or in relation to the information task.
F. Use a computer to generate modifiable flow charts, time lines, organizational charts, project plans (such as Gantt charts), and calendars which will help the student plan and organize complex or group information problem-solving tasks.
G. Use handheld devices such as personal digital assistants (PDAs), electronic slates or tablet PCs to track contacts and create to-do lists and schedules.

3. Location and Access

After students determine their priorities for information seeking, they must locate information from a variety of resources and access specific information found within individual resources. Students will be able to:

A. Locate and use appropriate computer resources and technologies available within the school library media center, including those on the library media center's local area network (e.g., online catalogs, periodical indexes, full-text sources, multimedia computer stations, CD-ROM stations, online terminals, scanners, digital cameras).
B. Locate and use appropriate computer resources and technologies available throughout the school including those available through intranets or local area networks (e.g., full-text resources, CD-ROMs, productivity software, scanners, digital cameras).
C. Locate and use appropriate computer resources and technologies available beyond the school through the Internet (e.g., newsgroups, listservs, WWW sites, ftp sites, online public access library catalogs, commercial databases and online services, and other community, academic, and government resources).
D. Know the roles and computer expertise of the people working in the school library media center and elsewhere who might provide information or assistance.
E. Use electronic reference materials (e.g., electronic encyclopedias, dictionaries, biographical reference sources, atlases, geographic databanks, thesauri, almanacs, fact books) available through intranets or local area networks, stand-alone workstations, commercial online vendors, or the Internet.
F. Use the Internet or commercial computer networks to contact experts and help and referral services.
G. Conduct self-initiated electronic surveys through e-mail, listservs, newsgroups and online data collection tools.
H. Use organizational systems and tools specific to electronic information sources that assist in finding specific and general information (e.g., indexes, tables of contents, user's instructions and manuals, legends, boldface and italics, graphic clues and icons, cross-references, Boolean logic strategies, time lines, hypertext links, knowledge trees, URLs, etc.) including the use of:

1. Search tools and commands for stand-alone, CD-ROM, networked or Web-based online databases and services;
2. Search tools and commands for searching the Internet, such as search engines, meta search tools, bots, directories, jump pages, and specialized resources such as those that search the Invisible Web;
3. Specialized sites and search tool commands that limit searches by date, location, format, collection of evaluated sites or other criteria.

4. Use of Information

After finding potentially useful resources, students must engage (read, view, listen) the information to determine its relevance and then extract the relevant information. Students will be able to:

A. Connect and operate the computer technology needed to access information, and read the guides and manuals associated with such tasks.
B. Know and be able to use the software and hardware needed to view, download, decompress and open documents, files, and programs from Internet sites and archives.
C. Copy and paste information from an electronic source into a personal document complete with proper citation.
D. Take notes and outline with a word processor, database, presentation or similar productivity program.
E. Record electronic sources of information and locations of those sources in order to properly cite and credit sources in footnotes, endnotes, and bibliographies.
F. Use electronic spreadsheets, databases, and statistical software to process and analyze statistical data.
G. Analyze and filter electronic information in relation to the task, rejecting information that is not relevant.
H. Save and backup data gathered to secure locations (floppy disk, personal hard drive space, RW-CD, online storage, flash memory, etc.)

5. Synthesis

Students must organize and communicate the results of the information problem-solving effort. Students will be able to:

A. Classify and group information using a word processor, database or spreadsheet.
B. Use word processing and desktop publishing software to create printed documents, applying

keyboard skills equivalent to at least twice the rate of handwriting speed.

C. Create and use computer-generated graphics and art in various print and electronic presentations.
D. Use electronic spreadsheet software to create original spreadsheets.
E. Generate charts, tables and graphs using electronic spreadsheets and other graphing programs.
F. Use database software to create original databases.
G. Use presentation software to create electronic slide shows and to generate overhead transparencies and slides.
H. Create and use projection devices to show hypermedia and multimedia productions with digital video, audio and links to HTML documents or other programs. Convert presentations for display as Web pages.
I. Create Web pages and sites using hypertext markup language (HTML) in a text document or using Web page creation tools and know the procedure for having these pages loaded to a Web server.
J. Use e-mail, ftp, groupware, and other telecommunications capabilities to publish the results of the information problem-solving activity.
K. Use specialized computer applications as appropriate for specific tasks, e.g., music composition software, computer-assisted drawing and drafting programs, mathematics modeling software, scientific measurement instruments, etc.
L. Properly cite and credit electronic sources (text, graphics, sound and video) of information within the product as well as in footnotes, endnotes, and bibliographies.

6. Evaluation

Evaluation focuses on how well the final product meets the original task (effectiveness) and the process of how well students carried out the information problem-solving process (efficiency). Students may evaluate their own work and process or be evaluated by others (i.e., classmates, teachers, library media staff, parents). Students will be able to:

A. Evaluate electronic presentations in terms of the content and format and design self-assessment tools to help them evaluate their own work for both content and format.
B. Use spell and grammar checking capabilities of word processing and other software to edit and revise their work.
C. Apply legal principles and ethical conduct related to information technology related to copyright and plagiarism.
D. Understand and abide by telecomputing etiquette when using e-mail, newsgroups, listservs and other Internet functions.
E. Understand and abide by acceptable use policies and other school rules in relation to use of the Internet and other electronic technologies.
F. Use e-mail, real-time communications (e.g., listservs, newsgroups, instant messaging services, chat rooms, IP telephony) desktop teleconferencing, and groupware on the Internet and local area networks to communicate with teachers and others regarding their performance on assignments, tasks, and information problems.
G. Thoughtfully reflect on the use of electronic resources and tools throughout the process.

The Big6™ Skills Approach to Information Problem Solving

© Eisenberg and Berkowitz 1987

The Big6™ is an information literacy curriculum, an information problem-solving process, and a set of skills which provide a strategy for effectively and efficiently meeting information needs. The Big6™ Skills approach can be used whenever students are in a situation, academic or personal, which requires information to solve a problem, make a decision or complete a task. This model is transferable to school, personal, and work applications, as well as all content areas and the full range of grade levels. When taught collaboratively with content area teachers in concert with content-area objectives, it serves to ensure that students are information literate.

The Big6™

1. Task Definition
1.1 Define the task (the information problem).
1.2 Identify information needed in order to complete the task (to solve the information problem).

2. Information Seeking Strategies
2.1 Brainstorm all possible sources.
2.2 Select the best sources.

3. Location and Access
3.1 Locate sources.
3.2 Find information within the sources.

4. Use of Information
4.1 Engage in the source (read, hear, view, touch).
4.2 Extract relevant information.

5. Synthesis
5.1 Organize information from multiple sources.
5.2 Present the information.

6. Evaluation
6.1 Judge the process (efficiency).
6.2 Judge the product (effectiveness).

References and Suggested Reading

American Association of School Librarians. (1995). Information literacy: A position paper on information problem solving. *Emergency Librarian*, 23 (2), 20-23. (EJ514998).

American Association of School Librarians. (1998). *Information literacy standards for student learning.* Chicago: American Library Association.

American Association of School Librarians & Association for Educational Communications and Technology. (1998). *Information power: Building partnerships for learning.* Chicago: American Library Association.

American Library Association. (2000). *Information literacy community partnerships toolkit.* Available online: <http://library.austin.cc.tx.us/staff/lnavarro/communitypartnerships/toolkit.html>

Association of College and Research Libraries. (2000). *Information literacy competency standards for higher education.* Available online: <http://www.ala.org/acrl/ilintro.html>

Bawden,D. (2001). Information and digital literacies: A review of concepts. *Journal of Documentation, 57* (2), 218-59. (EJ632998).

The Big6™ skills information problem-solving approach. [Online]. Available: <http://www.big6.com/>

Bruce, C. S. (1997). *Seven faces of information literacy.* Blackwood, South Australia: Auslib Press.

Bruce, C. S. (1997). *The seven faces of information literacy in higher education.* Available online: <http://www2.fit.qut.edu.au/InfoSys/bruce/inflit/faces/faces1.htm>

California Media and Library Educators Association Staff. (1993). *From library skills to information literacy: A handbook for the 21st century.* Englewood, CO: Libraries Unlimited, Inc.

Committee on Information Technology Literacy, National Research Council. (1999). *Being fluent with information technology.* Available online: <http://www.nap.edu/books/030906399X/html>

Doyle, C. S. (1994). *Information literacy in an information society: A concept for the information age.* Syracuse, NY: ERIC Clearinghouse on Information & Technology. (ED372763).

Eisenberg, M. B. (1999). *Essential skills for the information age: The Big6™ in action.* Video, 38 minutes. Worthington, Ohio: Linworth Publishing.

Eisenberg, M. B. (2001). Beyond the bells and whistles: Technology skills for a purpose. *MultiMedia Schools,* 8 (3), 44-48, 50-51. (EJ633043).

Eisenberg, M., & Berkowitz, B. (1988). *Curriculum initiative: An agenda and strategy for library media programs.* Norwood, NJ: Ablex. (ED296731).

Eisenberg, M. B., & Berkowitz, R. E. (1992). Information problem-solving: The Big6™ skills approach. *School Library Media Activities Monthly,* 8 (5), 27-29,37,42. (EJ438023).

Eisenberg M., & Berkowitz, R. E. (1997). The Big6™ and electronic resources: A natural fit. *Book Report,* 16 (2), 15, 22. (EJ550884).

Eisenberg, M. B., & Berkowitz, R. E. (1999). *Teaching information & technology skills: The Big6™ in elementary schools.* Worthington, Ohio: Linworth Publishing.

Eisenberg, M. B., & Berkowitz, R. E. (2000). *Teaching information & technology skills: The Big6™ in secondary schools.* Worthington, Ohio: Linworth Publishing.

Eisenberg, M. B., & Ely, D. P. (1993). Plugging into the "Net." *Emergency Librarian,* 21 (2), 8-16. (EJ471260).

Eisenberg, M. B., & Lowe, C. A. (1999). Call to action: Getting serious about libraries and information in education. *MultiMedia Schools,* 6 (2), 18-21. (EJ586238).

Eisenberg, M. B., & Spitzer, K. L. (1991). Information technology and services in schools. In M. E. Williams (Ed.), *Annual review of information science and technology,* Vol. 26. (pp. 243-285). Medford, NJ: Learned Information, Inc. (EJ 441 688).

Fulton, K. (1997). *Learning in the digital age: Insights into the issues. The skills students need for technological fluency.* Santa Monica, CA: Milken Family Foundation. Available online: <http://www.mff.org/pubs/ME164.pdf>

Garland, K. (1995). The information search process: A study of elements associated with meaningful research tasks. *School Libraries Worldwide,* 1 (1), 41-53. (EJ503407).

International Society for Technology in Education (ISTE). (2000). *National educational technology standards for students-connecting curriculum and technology.* Eugene, OR: International Society for Technology in Education.

Johnson, D. (1995a). Captured by the web: K-12 schools and the World Wide Web. *MultiMedia Schools,* 2 (2), 24-30. (EJ499841).

Johnson, D. (1995b). The new and improved school library: How one district planned for the future. *School Library Journal, 41* (6), 36-39. (EJ505448).

Johnson, D. (1995c). Student access to the Internet: Librarians and teachers working together to teach higher level survival skills. *Emergency Librarian, 22* (3), 8-12. (EJ497895).

Johnson, D. (1999a). A curriculum built not to last. *School Library Journal, 45* (4), 26-29. (EJ586404).

Johnson, D. (1999b). Implementing an information literacy curriculum: One district's story. *NASSP Bulletin, 83* (605), 53-61. (EJ585576).

Johnson, D. (2000). Information power: Building standards that are useful. *Teacher Librarian, 28* (2), 19-20. (EJ623553).

Johnson, D. (2001). *What gets measured gets done: A school library media and technology program self-study workbook.* (ED450809). Available online: <http://www.ericit.org/digests/>

Kasowitz, A. S. (2000). Using the Big6™ to teach and learn with the Internet. Worthington, Ohio: Linworth Publishing. (ED449781).

Klink, M.T. (1999). Resource-based learning. *Knowledge Quest, 27* (4), 26-30. (EJ588282).

Kuhlthau, C. C. (1993). Implementing a process approach to information skills: A study identifying indicators of success in library media programs. *School Library Media Quarterly, 22* (1), 11-18. (EJ473063).

Kuhlthau, C. C. (1995). The process of learning from information. *School Libraries Worldwide, 1* (1), 1-12. (EJ503404)

Loertscher, D. V., & Woolls, B. (2002). *Information literacy: A review of the research* (2nd ed.). Hillow Research and Publishing.

Mankato Schools Information Literacy Curriculum Guideline. [Online]. Available: <http://www.isd77.k12.mn.us/resources/infolit.html>

McKenzie, J. (2000). *Beyond technology: Questioning, research and the information literate school.* Bellingham, WA: FNO Press.

McNally, M. J., & Kulhthau, C. C. (1994). Information search process in science education. *Reference Librarian, 44,* 53-60. (EJ488273).

Minnesota Department of Education. (1989). *Model learner outcomes for educational media and technology.* St. Paul, MN: Minnesota Department of Education. (ED336070).

Moursund, D. (1995). Effective practices (part 2): Productivity tools. *Learning and Leading with Technology, 23* (4), 5-6.

Nuts and bolts of the Big6: In search of information literacy. [Online]. <http://www.kn.pacbell.com/wired/big6>

Pappas, M. L. (1993). A vision of school library media centers in an electronic information age. *School Library Media Activities Monthly, 10* (1), 32-34,38. (EJ469122).

Pappas, M. L. (1995). Information skills for electronic resources. *School Library Media Activities Monthly, 11* (8), 39-40. (EJ499875).

Potter, C. J. et al. (2000). *Information and technology literacy standards matrix.* Madison, WI: Wisconsin State Dept. of Public Instruction. (ED445663).

Rader, H. B. (1994). Information literacy and the undergraduate curriculum. *Library Trends, (44)* 2, 270-278.

Spitzer, K. S., Eisenberg, M. B., & Lowe, C. A. (1998). *Information literacy: Essential skills for the information age.* Syracuse, NY: ERIC Clearinghouse on Information & Technology. (ED427780).

Todd, R. J. (1995). Information literacy: Philosophy, principles, and practice. *School Libraries Worldwide,* 1 (1), 54-68. (EJ503408).

Todd, R. J. (1995). Integrated information skills instruction: Does it make a difference? *School Library Media Quarterly, 23* (2), 133-138. (EJ497921).

Todd, R. J. (1999). Transformational leadership and transformational learning: Information literacy and the World Wide Web. *NASSP Bulletin, 83* (605), 4-12. (EJ585570).

Wisconsin Educational Media Association. (1993). *Information literacy: A position paper on information problem-solving.* Madison, WI: WEMA Publications. (ED376817).

The Authors

Michael B. Eisenberg is Dean and Professor, University of Washington Information School.

Doug Johnson is Director of Media and Technology, Mankato Public Schools, Mankato, Minnesota.

This publication is funded in part with Federal funds from the U.S. Department of Education under contract number ED-99-CO-0005. The content of this publication does not necessarily reflect the views or policies of the U.S. Department of Education nor does mention of trade names, commercial products, or organizations imply endorsement by the U.S. government. Visit the Department of Education's Web site at:<http://www.ed.gov>.

Information Services—Including Technology

Resources Provision	Online catalogs, information retrieval, electronic resources (including CD-ROM nets), WWW/net resources, AskERIC, Internet Public Library, online discussion groups (listservs, newsgroups)
Direct Information Service	AskERIC, Internet Public Library, online discussion groups (listservs, newsgroups), LM_NET
Reading Guidance	Interactive CD-ROMs, collaborative projects on the Internet, e-mail, online discussion groups (listservs, newsgroups)
Curriculum Consultation/Development	E-mail, online discussion groups (listservs, newsgroups), AskERIC, collaborative projects on the Internet, groupware, production and presentation software/hardware

Part V: Instructional Design and Redesign

Instructional Design and Redesign

Introduction

Learning the Big6™ is cumulative, i.e., students gain proficiency in the process and skills over time. We also emphasize that the Big6™ Skills are best learned in two contexts: the context of the overall process itself, and within the context of real needs — curricular or personal.

Ensuring that students learn essential Big6™ Skills in these two contexts means designing learning events that help students to learn the overall Big6™ process as well as the individual Big6™ Skills. This "systematic instructional design" takes place on two levels:

1. The micro level—designing integrated instructional units and lessons.
2. The macro level—planning for integrated curriculum on the classroom, grade, subject area, or overall school level.

The activities, worksheets, and readings in Part V focus on the micro level. Developing skills in analysis and planning on the macro level is covered in Part VIII.

Micro Instructional Design

The goal in micro instructional design is to help classroom, library, and technology teachers learn to integrate Big6™ units and lessons. The subject area content of such units and lessons are provided within school- or classroom-defined curriculum. As part of any classroom learning experience, students must engage in various Big6™ information problem-solving stages. Students use the Big6™ whenever a teacher requires them to do the following:

- Listen to a lecture or video
- Conduct an experiment
- Read from a textbook
- Complete a worksheet
- Make a project
- Take a test
- Select a topic
- Do some homework

It is possible and highly desirable to weave Big6™ instruction throughout existing or planned classroom instruction. THE BIG6™ IS NOT AN ADD-ON! Instruction in the Big6™ is integrated with classroom instruction and is integral to success in completing subject area goals and objectives.

Curriculum—Big6™ Connection

The following activity sheet and worksheets focus attention on the curriculum-Big6™ connection. One key requirement for educators is to recognize the Big6™ Skills within units and lessons. To this end, the questions and forms help teachers (classroom, library, and technology) to decide upon (1) the important elements of instruction, (2) the key skills for student success as well as where they may have difficulties, and (3) the specifics of delivering integrated instruction through units and lessons.

Part V concludes with the ERIC Digest, "Motivation in Instructional Design," by Dr. Ruth Small. This Digest explains the ARCS Model of Motivational Design. ARCS stands for:

- Attention
- Relevance
- Confidence
- Satisfaction

We find that designing integrated units and lessons from an ARCS model guarantees effective Big6™ and content area learning.

Activity Sheet

This exercise will help you analyze the Collaborative Instructional Unit Planning Process.

Developing Big6™ Understandings

Worksheet 5-1—Integrated Curriculum Situation

Create a typical, integrated curriculum situation. Describe one or two activities that relate to each of the Big6™ Skills.

Big6™ Skills	Activities
1. Task Definition 1.1 Define the problem. 1.2 Identify the information needed.	
2. Information Seeking Strategies 2.1 Determine all possible sources. 2.2 Select the best source.	
3. Location & Access 3.1 Locate sources. 3.2 Find information within sources.	
4. Use of Information 4.1 Engage (e.g., read, hear, view). 4.2 Extract relevant information.	
5. Synthesis 5.1 Organize information from multiple sources. 5.2 Present the result.	
6. Evaluation 6.1 Judge the result (effectiveness). 6.2 Judge the process (efficiency).	

Unit & Lesson Implementation

Worksheet 5-2— Big6™ Unit Planning Guide

Teacher:	**Subject:**
Unit/Topic:	

Collaborative Instructional Unit Planning: Key Questions to Ask and Answer
1. What do we want students to know, do, and be like when they finish this unit of study?
2. What are the content area objectives?
3. What are the Big6™ Skills objectives?
4. Where does this fit into the overall curriculum?
5. What will students do to demonstrate their new knowledge or skill?
6. How will the instructional unit be managed? (grouping, time frame, materials, and so on)?

Worksheet 5-3—
Big6™ Unit Planning Guide

Teacher: **Subject:**

Unit/Topic:

Big6™ Skills	Collaborative Instructional Planning Guide: Activities	Level of Instruction	LMS and/or Teacher	Focus
1. Task Definition 1.1 Define the problem. 1.2 Identify the information needed.				
2. Information Seeking Strategies 2.1 Determine all possible sources. 2.2 Select the best source.				
3. Location & Access 3.1 Locate sources. 3.2 Find information within sources.				
4. Use of Information 4.1 Engage (e.g., read, hear, view). 4.2 Extract relevant information.				
5. Synthesis 5.1 Organize information from multiple sources. 5.2 Present the result.				
6. Evaluation 6.1 Judge the result (effectiveness). 6.2 Judge the process (efficiency)				

Worksheet 5-4—Instructional Unit Design Format

Unit:
Audience:

Overview:
Rationale:
Subject Area Objectives:
Big6™ Objectives:
Activities:
Evaluation:
Materials:
Follow-up/Supplemental Activities:

Worksheet 5-5— Lesson Plan Format

Subject:	**Teacher:**
Lesson Name:	**Location:**
Class:	**Unit Context:**
Date:	

Activities	**Big6™ Skills**	**Subject/Area Objectives**

Materials/Resources:

Evaluation:

Notes:

Worksheet 5-6— Generic Lesson Plan Format

Title:		

Grade Level	Related Big6™ Skills	Purpose

Learning Contexts:

Discussion:

Sample in Context:

Plagiarism

Plagiarism

Help!

"What can we do to stop students from just copying and pasting and presenting the work as their own?"

Fighting Plagiarism

- **Work separately on Use of Information and Synthesis before requiring that both be done together.**
  - Have students provide "direct quote" answers before requiring them to do so in their own words.
  - Give students the "direct quote" answers and then have them put the direct quotes in their own words.
  - Do not advance until students can do each of these skills successfully on their own.

Fighting Plagiarism

- **Create a culture that promotes "citing in context."**
  - Have students learn to cite at an early age.
  - Model citing in teachers' work.
  - Show "bad" examples—exaggerate plagiarism.
  - Have students cite all sources all the time.
  - Do not accept work without citing.
  - Expect citing in class discussions as well.

Fighting Plagiarism

Ask good questions.

- Assignments that are simply "descriptive" are easily copied.
- Assignments that ask students to make judgments or defend a position require thinking and are not easily copied.

DESCRIPTIVE	INFERENTIAL
Do a report on a U.S. state.	Your family is considering moving to another state. Based on research about this state, decide whether you think it's a good idea.
Write a paper on humpback whales.	Write a paper on whether hump-back whales are still endangered should or should not be protected.

ERIC Clearinghouse on Information
& Technology at Syracuse University
621 Skytop Road, Suite 160
Syracuse, New York 13244
www.ericit.org
EDO-IR-2002-04

ERIC Digest

ERIC Digest—Motivation in Instructional Design

by Ruth V. Small

Introduction

Developing life-long learners who are intrinsically motivated, display intellectual curiosity, find learning enjoyable, and continue seeking knowledge after their formal instruction has ended has always been a major goal of education. Early motivational research was conducted primarily in the workplace, and centered on ways to motivate industrial workers to work harder, faster, and better.

More recent motivational research focuses on the identification of effective techniques for enhancing instructional design, improving classroom management, and meeting the needs of diverse student populations (Wlodkowski, 1981). Learning-motivation researchers are applying some of the same theories and concepts found to be effective in industry to the development of motivational models that enhance the teaching-learning environment. One such model is the ARCS Model of Motivational Design developed by John M. Keller of Florida State University (Keller, 1983, 1987). ARCS is a systematic model for designing motivating instruction. This digest will describe the ARCS Model, and will outline some of the ways in which ARCS components may be applied to instructional design.

The ARCS Model of Motivational Design

The ARCS Model of Motivational Design is a well-known and widely applied model of instructional design. Simple, yet powerful, the ARCS Model is rooted in a number of motivational theories and concepts, (see Keller, 1983) most notably expectancy-value theory (e.g. Vroom, 1964; Porter and Lawler, 1968).

In expectancy-value theory, "effort" is identified as the major measurable motivational outcome. For "effort" to occur, two necessary prerequisites are specified: (1) the person must value the task and (2) the person must believe he or she can succeed at the task. Therefore, in an instructional situation, the learning task needs to be presented in a way that is engaging and meaningful to the student, and in a way that promotes positive expectations for the successful achievement of learning objectives.

The ARCS Model identifies four essential strategy components for motivating instruction:

[A]ttention strategies for arousing and sustaining curiosity and interest;

[R]elevance strategies that link to learners' needs, interests, and motives;

[C]onfidence strategies that help students develop a positive expectation for successful achievement; and

[S]atisfaction strategies that provide extrinsic and intrinsic reinforcement for effort (Keller, 1983).

Keller (1987) breaks each of the four ARCS components down into three strategy sub-components. The strategy sub-components and instructionally relevant examples are shown below.

Attention

Perceptual Arousal: provide novelty, surprise, incongruity or uncertainty. Ex. The teacher places a sealed box covered with question marks on a table in front of the class.

Inquiry Arousal: stimulate curiosity by posing questions or problems to solve. Ex. The teacher presents a scenario of a problem situation and asks the class to brainstorm possible solutions based on what they have learned in the lesson.

Variability: incorporate a range of methods and media to meet students' varying needs. Ex. After displaying and reviewing each step in the process on the overhead projector, the teacher divides the class into teams and assigns each team a set of practice problems.

Relevance

Goal Orientation: present the objectives and useful purpose of the instruction and specific methods for successful achievement. Ex. The teacher explains the objectives of the lesson.

Motive Matching: match objectives to student needs and motives. Ex. The teacher allows the students to present their projects in writing or orally to accommodate different learning needs and styles.

Familiarity: present content in ways that are understandable and that are related to the learners' experience and values. Ex. The teacher asks the students to provide examples from their own experiences for the concept presented in class.

Confidence

Learning Requirements: inform students about learning and performance requirements and assessment criteria. Ex. The teacher provides students with a list of assessment criteria for their research projects and circulates examples of exemplary projects from past years.

Success Opportunities: provide challenging and meaningful opportunities for successful learning. Ex. The teacher allows the students to practice extracting and summarizing information from various sources and then provides feedback before the students begin their research projects.

Personal Responsibility: link learning success to students' personal effort and ability. Ex. The teacher provides written feedback on the quality of the students' performance and acknowledges the students' dedication and hard work.

Satisfaction

Intrinsic Reinforcement: encourage and support intrinsic enjoyment of the learning experience. Ex. The teacher invites former students to provide testimonials on how learning these skills helped them with subsequent homework and class projects.

Extrinsic Rewards: provide positive reinforcement and motivational feedback. Ex. The teacher awards certificates to students as they master the complete set of skills.

Equity: maintain consistent standards and consequences for success. Ex. After the term project has been completed, the teacher provides evaluative feedback using the criteria described in class.

Motivation Assessment Instruments

Since the ARCS Model was introduced in the early 1980s, several instruments have been developed for assessing the motivational quality of instructional situations. The Instructional Materials Motivation Survey (IMMS) (Keller, 1987) asks students to rate 36 ARCS-related statements in relation to the instructional materials they have just used. Some examples are:

"These materials are eye-catching." (Attention)
"It is clear to me how the content of this material is related to things I already know." (Relevance)
"As I worked on this lesson, I was confident that I could learn the content." (Confidence)
"Completing the exercises in this lesson gave me a satisfying feeling of accomplishment." (Satisfaction)

Keller and Keller (1989) developed the Motivational Delivery Checklist, a 47-item ARCS-based instrument for evaluating the motivational characteristics of an instructor's classroom delivery. Examples of items related to each ARCS component are:

"Uses questions to pose problems or paradoxes." (Attention)
"Uses language and terminology appropriate to learners and their context." (Relevance)
"Provides feedback on performance promptly." (Confidence)
"Makes statements giving recognition and credit to learners as appropriate." (Satisfaction)

The Web site Motivational Analysis Checklist (WebMAC) (Small,1997) is an instrument used for designing and assessing the motivational quality of World Wide Web sites. WebMAC builds on Keller's work (1987a; 1987b; 1989), Taylor's Value-Added Model (1986), and the research on relevance and information retrieval (e.g. Schamber, 1994). Still in development and testing, WebMAC identifies 60 items that are categorized according to four general characteristics: Engaging, Meaningful, Organized, and Enjoyable. Some examples of items are:

"Eye-catching title and/or visual on home page." (Engaging)
"User-controlled type of information accessed." (Meaningful)
"Logical sequence of information." (Organized)
"Links to other Web sites of interest." (Enjoyable)

Summary

The ARCS Model of Motivational Design is an easy-to-apply, heuristic approach to increasing the motivational appeal of instruction. ARCS provides a useful framework for both the design and improvement of the motivational quality of a range of informational entities - from classroom instruction to Internet resources - and increases the likelihood that these entities will be used and enjoyed.

References and Related Readings

Chemotti, J.T. (1992, June). From nuclear arms to Hershey's kisses: Strategies for motivating students. *School Library Media Activities Monthly*, 8(10), 34-36. (EJ 446 223)

Keller, J.M.(1983). Motivational design of instruction. In C.M. Reigeluth (Ed.). *Instructional design theories and models: An overview of their current status.* Hillsdale, NJ: Erlbaum.

Keller, J.M. (1987a, Oct.). Strategies for stimulating the motivation to learn. *Performance and Instruction*, 26(8), 1-7. (EJ 362 632)

Keller, J.M. (1987b). IMMS: Instructional materials motivation survey. Florida State University.

Keller, J.M. & Keller, B.H. (1989). Motivational delivery checklist. Florida State University.

Porter, L.W. & Lawler, E.E. (1968). *Managerial attitudes and performance.* Homewood, IL: Dorsey Press.

Schamber, L. (1994). *Relevance and information behavior. Annual Review of Information Science and Technology*. Medford, NJ: Learned Information, Inc. (EJ 491 620)

Small, R.V. (1992, Apr.). Taking AIM: Approaches to instructional motivation. *School Library Media Activities Monthly*, 8(8), 32-34.

Small, R.V. (1997). Assessing the motivational quality of world wide Web sites. ERIC Clearinghouse on Information and Technology. (ED 407 930, IR 018 331)

Taylor, R.S. (1986). *Value-added processes in information systems.* Norwood, NJ: Ablex. (ISBN: 0-89391-273-5)

Vroom, V.H. (1964). *Work and motivation.* New York: Wiley.

Wlodkowski, R.J. (1981). Making sense out of motivation: A systematic model to consolidate motivational constructs across theories. *Educational Psychologist, 16*(2), 101-110.

• • • • •

This ERIC Digest was prepared by Ruth V. Small, associate professor of Information Studies at Syracuse University, Syracuse, New York.

ERIC Clearinghouse on Information & Technology, Syracuse University, 621 Skytop Rd. Suite 160, Syracuse, New York 13244-4100; (315) 443-3640; (800) 464-9107; Fax: (315) 443-5448; E-mail: eric@ericir.syr.edu; URL: <http://ericit.org/>

This publication was prepared with funding from the Office of Educational Research and Improvement, U.S. Department of Education under contract no. RR93002009. The opinions expressed in this report do not necessarily reflect the positions of OERI or ED.

Activate a Big6™ Tool to Improve Learning (Grades 7–12)

by Bob Berkowitz

Here is a recipe for improvement. It's a twist on an old idea. Maybe you have used a "KWL" graphic organizer before, but one Big6™ modification links a series of questions to your research goal. To the old "KWL" Chart, simply add an "H." That one change can turn an old idea into a new, best strategy when you need to make sense of your task and organize a lot of information—it's now a "KWHL" Chart.

K—Stands for what you KNOW about the subject.
W—Stands for determining what you WANT to learn.
H—Stands for HOW you can learn more (sources where additional information on the topic can be found).
L—Stands for identifying what you LEARN as you read.

The KWHL Chart is a simple, yet effective organizer that you can use for planning and gathering information. Specifically, the KWHL Chart is useful when you need to access prior information on a topic or theme, identify needed primary and secondary resources, develop a plan for accessing resources, identify attributes and characteristics to research, and take notes on what you are learning.

The KWHL Chart is an excellent tool that you can use as a plan for investigation. A KWHL inquiry chart can include questions about predictions and/or implications. Additionally, these charts can be used as a basis to formulate a hypothesis, or research question, with confirmation refutation as your research progresses.

Throughout the research process add information to your KWHL Chart. One trick you may want to try is to use different color marking pens each time you add information to the chart. This technique will give you a visual representation of the knowledge acquired throughout your research experience.

An example of a KWHL Chart has these headings:

- What we know about _______?
- What we want to learn about _____?
- How can I find information about ______?
- What we learned about _____?
- How this relates to us?

Other questions you can ask in a matrix format are shown in the example below.

- What do I already know?
- What do I want to find out?
- How am I going to find out?
- What did I learn?

What do I already know?	What do I want to find out?	How am I going to find out?	What did I learn?

Know Your Information Sources (Grades 7–12)

by Susan McMullen

Related Information Literacy Skills: Big6™ #2—Information Seeking Strategies

Purpose: To help students recognize various information sources and to apply appropriate criteria for selecting the best information source(s) for their particular research need.

Learning Contexts: The lesson is applicable for tasks that involve any type of information seeking, research, or report writing in secondary and higher education settings.

Discussion: When confronted with a research project, students are frequently either overwhelmed by or uninformed about their information source choices. Today's students frequently equate information seeking with the World Wide Web. They do not realize that there are a wide variety of information choices available to them, each requiring different finding methods. This exercise will help students identify different sources of information, their quality and content, and understand how they are organized. By understanding the various types of information and where information comes from, students will recognize appropriate sources for specific seeking or research topics.

Sample in Context: This lesson begins with a brainstorming activity in which the instructor asks the students to identify different information sources. If the class is small, each student may be asked to give one source. The instructor and students then review the "Know Your Information Sources" handout to get familiar with the major resources. Once familiar with these major resources, students are asked to complete the "What Source Would You Use" exercise. After this initial preparation, students are then asked to apply appropriate selection criteria to their information task.

Item: Know Your Information Sources
Using the "Know Your Information Sources" handout, determine the best information source(s) to use in the situations presented in the "What Source Would You Use" exercise. Upon completing the exercise, think about your own information task. As you prepare for research, think about the questions on the bottom half of the exercise sheet. Your answers will help you determine the most useful sources for locating information on your topic.

Know Your Information Sources

by Susan McMullen

What Source Would You Use?

N=Newspaper, PM=Popular Magazine, SJ=Scholarly Journal, R=Reference Book, B=Book, W=Web, P=Person

Hint: You may select more than one source.

______ to find statistics on the number of working mothers with children under the age of five

______ to locate an in-depth article about the level of absenteeism among working mothers with children under the age of five

______ to find out information about the day care center that XYZ corporation opened in your home town

______ to learn about presentations offered at the National Association for Family Child Care Conference in July 2003

______ to find current analysis of how working mothers in the 21st century are coping with child care issues

______ to find out how much families are paying for child care

______ to read a detailed analysis of child-care options in the workplace

______ to learn about companies that are offering child care at the workplace

Diamond Thinking (Grades 6-12)

by Bob Berkowitz

Related Big6™ Skills: Big6™ #4—Use of Information

Purpose: In this activity, students associate their ideas with the information they find.

Learning Contexts: Grades 6–12. Diamond Thinking is an Information Use strategy that helps students become divergent thinkers. This activity encourages students to expand their ideas as they engage and extract information from material they read, hear, or view.

Discussion: Ask students to list information from their research in the "Information" diamond (left diamond). Students then respond to that information by writing their thoughts in the "My Thoughts" diamond (right diamond). Information in the "My Thoughts" diamond may be based upon personal opinion or experience. In addition, students may fill in the "My Thoughts" with questions that were not answered by information they read, heard, or viewed.

Variation: One variation is to switch the headings and make "My Thoughts" in the left diamond, and "Information" in the right column. Using this variation, students begin by listing their ideas and opinions, and through research, complete the right diamond with information that validates or disputes their opinion.

Item: Diamond Thinking handout

Sample in Context:
Students in Mr. Lake's 12th grade health class are working on a communicable diseases unit. Mr. Lake's assignment includes accessing and locating information on the Web about communicable diseases. To help students personalize the experience, he uses the "Diamond Thinking" strategy.

As students locate and read Web-based information on their topics from the pre-selected sites, they complete the left diamond with four facts that relate to how the disease is transmitted. These facts are placed in the "Information" diamonds.

Students respond with their opinion or personal experience in the corresponding right "My Thoughts" diamond. In this way, students are able to provide their own strategies about preventing the spread of communicable diseases.

As an extension of this assignment, students may continue their research to determine the effectiveness or viability of their recommendations. Students proceed down the Diamond Thinking handout until they've completed their assignment. It is easy to see how Diamond Thinking can act as a springboard for a variety of extension activities.

Diamond Thinking Handout

by Robert E. Berkowitz

While you're researching your topic, use the graphic organizer below to record and think about what you've read, heard, or viewed. This exercise will help you become a divergent thinker and will help you expand your ideas as you gather (engage and extract) information from sources.

1. In the "Information" diamond below, list facts you've read, heard, or viewed about your topic.
2. In the "My Thoughts" diamond, list your thoughts, feelings, experiences, or unanswered questions that relate to your facts in the "Information" diamond.

Topic:____

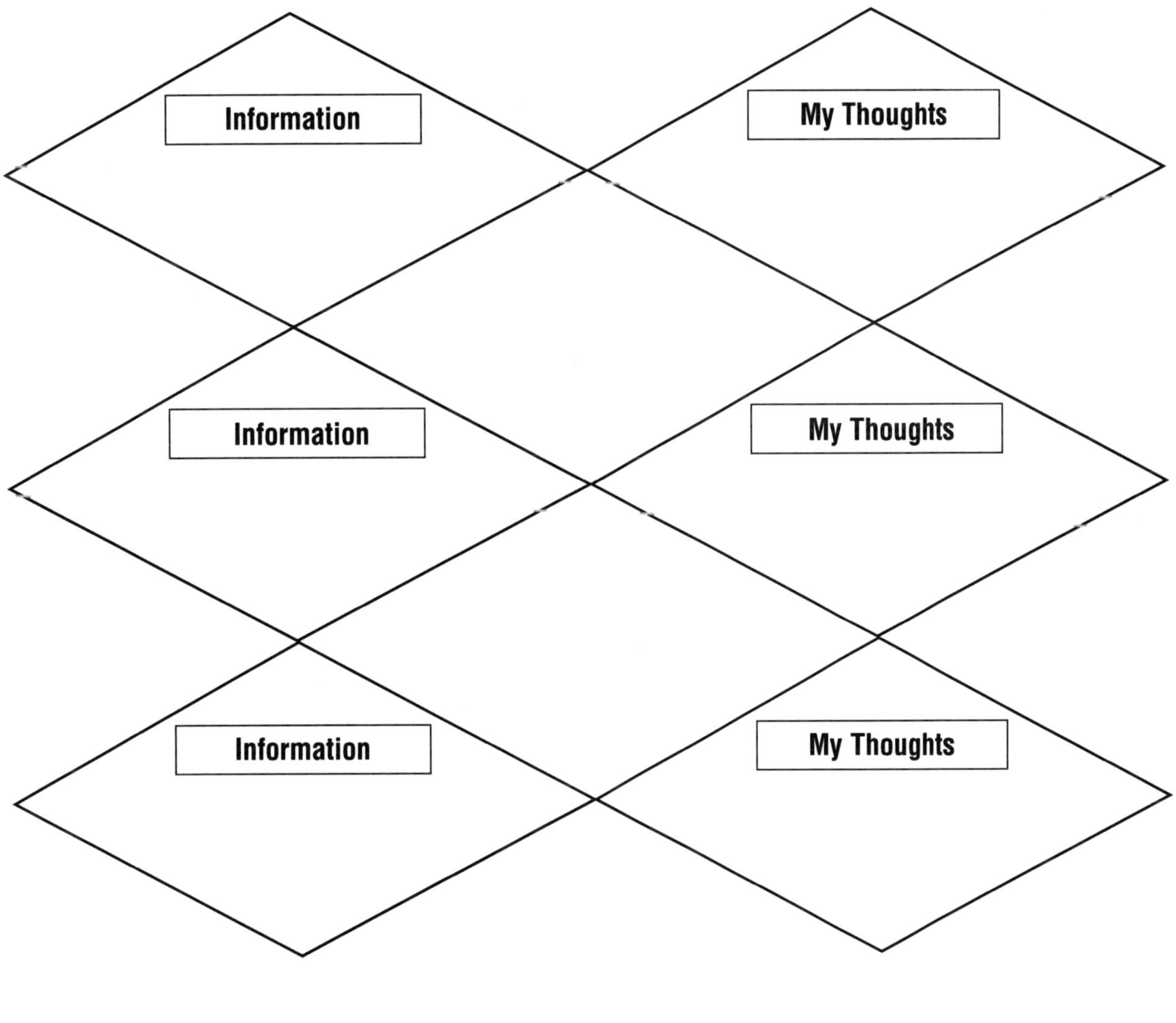

Think Sheet

Part VI: Assessment

The Big6™ Assessment

Introduction

- Have students learned what was intended?
- Are students proficient in the overall Big6™ process?
- Are students able to solve information problems across a range of situations, subjects, and settings?
- Are students skilled in each of the Big6™ stages and sub-stages?

Answering these questions is what assessment is all about. Assessment is often dreaded because it comes across as negative and difficult to accomplish. This need not be the case. Assessment can be used to recognize strengths and highlight skills that need improving, and assessment can be handled in a straight-forward manner. We emphasize that teachers should communicate expectations as well as the techniques that will be used to evaluate student performance in relation to expectations. The evidence required to assess Big6™ proficiency can be gathered within the context of existing assignments, tests, products, and other forms of assessment.

Assess the Process

Assessment from a Big6™ perspective means going beyond simply whether the students learned the content that was taught. Teachers must also determine students' abilities in terms of the processes involved. For example, it is important to know whether students were able to clearly articulate their assignment and the information needed (Task Definition) or whether they were able to acquire the information they were supposed to get (Information Seeking Strategies and Location & Access). And, could they pull out the valuable information and apply it to the task (Use of Information and Synthesis)? Lastly, were the students themselves able to recognize and correct deficiencies in their work (Evaluation)? In other words, classroom teachers and teacher-librarians must be able to assess performance within the information problem-solving process itself and then develop ways for students to address deficiencies and problems.

Self Assessment

We also believe that assessment is the responsibility of students as well as teachers. Students must be able to assess the results of their efforts by analyzing the effectiveness of their products and their efficient use of the information problem-solving strategy. It is crucial to help students learn to:

- Value and recognize quality work
- Reflect on the ways they go about tackling assignments and tasks
- Determine how they can improve
- Recognize the relationship between self-discipline and achievement
- Gain self-confidence in solving information problems

Students frequently have no idea why they scored as they did on an assignment. At best, they might speculate on what they did wrong. It's more likely that they won't even think about it. Students must be encouraged to assume ownership of their own work through self-assessment. Students can and must also learn this process of assessment. They need to know how to identify the factors that define a job well done, determine whether they found all of them, and compare their products with an exemplar.

But that is not enough. Students must then gauge whether they were properly engaged in the process. They should be able to determine whether they were efficient in terms of time management, product development, or even assessment. Additionally, students must develop skills in judging their effectiveness. They need to know that they can recognize an exemplar when presented with one.

It's important to take the guesswork out of assessment. If a student judges his or her work to be "good or excellent," but the teacher rates it as just "fair or adequate," there's a gap between teacher and student understanding—and that's a clear problem. In learning and using the Big6™, we hope that students and teachers can eliminate that gap. This can happen by helping students learn to assess their own products and skills according to the same criteria that teachers use. We talk about having students think like their teachers or "getting inside their teachers' heads." Students can learn to assume ownership for their own learning, to diagnose problems, and to select solutions.

The exercise in Part VI of the Workshop Handbook is designed to help educators develop competence in assessing students' Big6™ abilities. The aids—particularly the Big6™ Scoring Guides—are useful mechanisms for documenting and planning assessment criteria and evidence.

For example, Bob's in-service workshop on assessment is built around the "Postcard" Assessment Exercise. Bob asks the teachers to analyze the assignment from a Big6™ perspective. What is required of the students? What are the key Big6™ Skills? What criteria will be used to assess student performance? Bob and the teachers (sometimes working in groups) then start to fill in the Big6™ Scoring Guide matrix:

1. First, members need to agree upon a grading scale (e.g., "Highly Competent to Not Yet Acceptable").
2. Next, members discuss which stages of the Big6™ are represented or emphasized in the assignment in some way. They determine the "degree of focus" for each Big6™ Skill to be assessed and assign a relative percentage in the rightmost column.
3. Then teachers define the criteria within each Big6™ Skill and level, for example, whatever the "best case" would be for Task Definition becomes the expectation for Highly Competent. Bob and the teachers work through each level down to "Not Yet Acceptable."
4. The matrix is completed by determining what evidence will be used to assess student performance. They go through each of the Big6™ trying to determine the qualities and quantities of work expected and the evidence required to measure the work. Last, the weight or percent of focus is finalized.

After the Scoring Guide is defined, the teachers break into groups to assess the postcards. They gain experience applying their assessment tool to actual student work. Debriefing includes discussing the value and approaches to assessing both the Big6™ process and the final products of student work.

The article on Big6™ Scoring Guides is from *The Big6™ Newsletter*. It provides further explanation about the various forms and how to use them.

Assessment Exercise

Worksheet 6-1—Data Collection Sheet (Blank)

Worksheet 6-2—Postcard Assessment Exercise

Review the following instructional activity. Determine the Big6™ Skills attributes, focus, and criteria to assess student performance.

You have just won the grand prize in the Spanish 2 Cultural Sweepstakes. The prize is an all expenses paid trip to South America, Central America, or Spain. Because Mrs. Hoffman is a terrific teacher, you have decided to write her two postcards to describe your trip.

Your task is to write two picture postcards, either from a Spanish-speaking country in South America, Central America, or from Spain. One card's content should focus on topics from the "social" list below and the second card should focus on topics from the "political" list below.

The front of each postcard must have a graphic (picture or drawing) that illustrates the content of the written message.

Social:	**Political:**
______ recreation	______ government structure
______ clothing	______ history
______ celebrations	______ currency
______ customs and traditions	______ employment
______ sports/games	______ climate
______ food	______ regions (beaches, mountains, and the like)
______ communication	______ historical personalities
______ religion	______ population statistics
______ family life	______ exports/imports
______ school	______ sites of interests/places to visit
______ art	______ current events
______ shopping	______ historical landmarks
______ housing	
______ music	
______ entertainment	

Assessment Exercise (cont.)

Assessment Exercise (cont.)

Dear Mrs. Hoffman,

Madnd is great! shopping here is excellent. The malls here are gigantic and beautiful (See front) Most malls have more than 150 stores. Madrid is called the "capitol of joy and contentment." our tour guide told us that the UN had to invent the word 'la movida' to describe Madrid's bustling nightlife! Madrid's restaurants offer a variety of food from around the world. The city's most popular dish is Madrid Stew. Some of ingredients are potatoes, chickpeas, black pudding and meat. There are more than 140 art galleries in Madrid. Every year, there is a contemporary Art Fair. It is one of the most important art fairs in the world. Well, I have to go. We're going to an open-air cafe for lunch. See you soon!

Katie

Mrs Hoffman
6200 Ontario Ctr. R
Ontario, NY
14520

Dear Mrs Hoffman,

Hi! I'm in Madrid. yesterday, I visited the Plaza Mayor. It is the sight for many things such as: bullfights, dances, concerts, and fairs. Every Sunday, there is a stamp and coin show. There is a place in Madrid called 'zero kilometre'. It has been there ever since the 19th century. It is the distance marker for all the roads leading out of the city. My tour guide told me that the population of Madrid is about 3,124,000. That's almost three times the population of Barcelona! I was also told about Spain's exports. They are citrus fruits, olive oil, wine, footwear, and vegetables. I have to go now. We're going to the park for a picnic See you later!

Katie

Mrs. Hoffman
6300 Ontario Ctr. Rd
Ontario, NY
14520

Assessment Exercise (cont.)

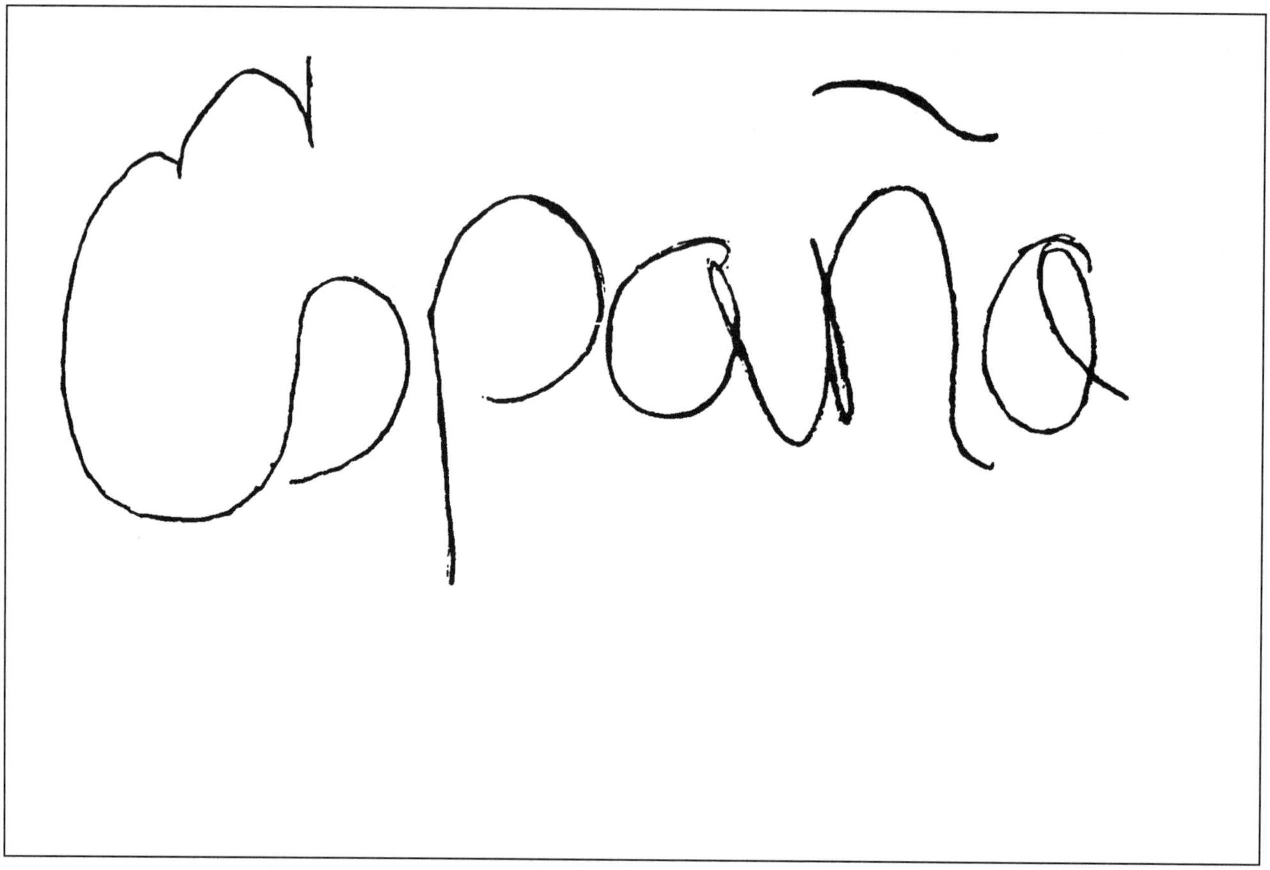

Assessment Exercise (cont.)

Dear Mrs. Hoffman,

Brazil is very hot and humid. I was very tired when I got in my hotel room. And that was only one minute after I got out of my "El Taxi!" It is so boring here, I miss Panama! The only thing I liked about this country is the weather at night...........

Hasta Luego

Sarah

Mrs. Hoffman
6200 ont. centr. Rd
ont. centr. N.Y
14568

Dear Mrs. Hoffmann,

Ohhh man...I just love those malls. They are humongous. They have 76 stores. One of them is all souvenirs and party gifts, another is a history store with ancient jewels and other old stuff. Of course I'm talking about Brazil. I started to like it when I got used to the weather. Now I love this place................

C-Ya Later,

SARAH

Mrs. Hoffman
6200 ont. centr. rd
Ont. centr. N.Y 14568

Assessment: Big6™ Scoring Guides for Diagnosis and Prescription

by Bob Berkowitz

Big6™ Scoring Guides are designed to communicate expectations for students' work and achievement in ways that students can understand and use. Big6™ Scoring Guides focus on the process of solving information problems as well as the final result. Therefore, guides are useful both during and after working on assignments—for both formative and summative assessment.

Formative assessment, as explained in previous articles, involves diagnosing students' performances during learning so that adjustments can be made before students turn in their work. Adjustments may include:

- redirecting planned instruction to focus on areas where students are having trouble
- providing special learning activities not previously planned
- helping students to apply relevant technology tools
- redefining the problem or returning to a previous Big6™ stage
- offering one-on-one tutoring
- brainstorming alternative approaches

These types of adjustments are prescriptions for improving learning. Of course, Big6™ Scoring Guides can also be used to assess final products—summative assessment. In working with teachers, we find that post-assignment debriefings—built around Big6™ Scoring Guides—are effective ways of involving students in the assessment process.

To create Big6™ Scoring Guides

1. Define the curriculum objectives within a Big6™ context.
2. Determine which Big6™ Skills are important (the focus) for this particular assignment.
3. Develop criteria across a scale (from "highly competent" to "not yet acceptable"). There may be more than one aspect to each criteria. Consider which aspects are essential.
4. Determine what evidence will be examined to determine student performance for each Big6™ skill.
5. Conduct the assessment.
6. Share the assessment with students.
7. Revise as necessary.

Figure A: Muscular Action Worksheet

Your task is to design a controlled experiment to test the hypothesis below. Your experiment should be designed so that it can be conducted in a 15 to 20 minute period.

Hypothesis:
When there is an increase in muscular activity, there is a corresponding increase in the energy used by muscles. This energy increase causes heat as well as a corresponding increase in oxygen consumption.

Material:

Procedure:

Result: (tabulate data and represent in an appropriate graph)

Conclusion:

Questions:

- What variable(s) did you test?
- What are the constants?
- What is the experimental control?
- Evaluation/Scoring Guide

For example, assume that completing Figure A is the task for students in ninth-grade biology studying "muscular activity." Figure B is the Big6™ Scoring Guide designed to assess students' performance. This guide is designed to include multiple assessments by student (S), teacher (T), and library media specialist (L). This allows students and teachers to quickly identify gaps in their views of perceived performance. Focusing on gaps can lead to clarification of misunderstandings and highlighting the need for further instruction.

The column labeled "Evidence" indicates the products or techniques used to assess specific skills. Examples of evidence include written, visual, or oral products, assignments, homework, projects, tests, observation, or even self-reflection. This is an essential piece of the Scoring Guide since it identifies the specific context for assessing student performance.

The last column, "Focus," relates to the relative importance of each skill being evaluated. It is not necessary or desirable to assess all Big6™ skills equally in every learning situation. The assigned focus should be based on the goals and objectives of the unit in terms of Big6™ skill development and content learning. For example, in the muscle example, a percentage of emphasis is assigned to each of the Big6™ skills. Location & Access is not a skill emphasized in this situation while Task Definition, Information Seeking Strategy, and Synthesis are.

Figure C is an elementary curriculum example that uses a Big6™ Scoring Guide in context. The curriculum context is a science lab experiment on the effects of light on seed growth. The Scoring Guide is an easy way to compare student and teacher assessment on key Big6™ Skills: Location & Access, Use of Information, and Synthesis.

Figure B: Big6 Scoring Guide for Muscular Action

Big6™ Assessment Scoring Guide—Muscular Exercise

Big6™ Skills Eisenberg/Berkowitz © 1988		Highly Competent 10 points		Competent 8 points		Adequate 7 points		Not Yet Acceptable 5 points	Evidence	Focus
1. Task Definition 1.1 Define the problem. 1.2 Identify the information needed.	S T L	Experiment meets 15–20 minute requirement. Procedure tested: oxygen consumption and levels of heat.	S T L	Experiment limited to15–20 min. requirement. Procedure tested: oxygen consumption or levels of heat.	S T L	Experiment did not meet time requirement. Procedure tested: oxygen consumption or levels of heat, but not both.	S T L	Experiment did not meet time requirement. Procedure did not test for either: oxygen consumption or levels of heat.	Experiment	20%
2. Information Seeking Strategies 2.1 Determine all possible sources. 2.2 Select the best source.	S T L	Procedure can be repeated exactly and produce the same results. Procedure tests the hypothesis.	S T L	Procedure tested the hypothesis but is not easily followed.	S T L	Procedure tests the hypothesis but is not easily followed and does not give the same results.	S T L	Procedure does not test the hypothesis. Procedure cannot be repeated at all.	Procedure	40%
3. Location & Access 3.1 Locate sources. 3.2 Find information within sources.	S T L		S T L		S T L		S T L			
4. Use of Information 4.1 Engage (e.g., read, hear, view). 4.2 Extract relevant information.	S T L	Complete and accurate data tables. Complete and accurate graphs.	S T L	Accurate data tables. Appropriate but incomplete graphs.	S T L	Incomplete data tables. Incomplete and inaccurate graphs.	S T L	No data tables. No graphs.	Results	10%
5. Synthesis 5.1 Organize information from multiple sources. 5.2 Present the result.	S T L	Appropriate conclusion. Answers all questions completely.	S T L	Appropriate conclusion. Answers all questions poorly.	S T L	Conclusion attempted but is inappropriate. Questions poorly answered and/or only some questions answered.	S T L	No conclusion. No questions answered.	Conclusion Question	20%
6. Evaluation 6.1 Judge the result (effectiveness). 6.2 Judge the process (efficiency).	S T L	Scoring Guide thoughtfully completed.	S T L		S T L		S T L	Scoring Guide was not completed.	Scoring Guide	10%

(S) Student, (T) Teacher, (L) Library Media Specialist

The hardest part of creating Big6™ Scoring Guides is writing the specific statements of performance under each criteria and Big6™ skill. We find that people get much better at this over time. Figure D is provided as a template to help you practice.

We also find that collaboration helps. Try working with library media specialists, other teachers, and even students. In fact, having students participate in creating their own Big6™ Scoring Guides is an excellent technique for teaching the Big6™ Skills of Task Definition and Evaluation.

Figure C: Elementary Science Experiment: Light and Seed Growth

Objectives:

1. To study the impact of light on seed growth.
2. To gather necessary materials and conduct an experiment.
3. To keep a daily journal of observations.
4. To write up a lab and draw logical conclusions.

Procedures:

Working in pairs, students are to:

1. Line two glasses with paper towels and stuff the inside of the glasses with more paper towels to hold the paper towel liner against the glass.
2. Place four bean seeds, evenly spaced and half-way down, between the glass and the paper towels.
3. Dampen the paper towels with water.
4. Put one glass in a dark cupboard or cabinet and place the other glass on a windowsill.
5. Each day, moisten the paper towels in each glass.
6. Make observations in a journal each day for seven days. Note date, time, actions taken, observations.
7. Write up the experiment in scientific lab format. Include a written summary of results and a conclusion based on observations.

Assessment: Big6™ Scoring Guide for Light and Seed Growth Experiment

Big6™ Skills	Expert Scientist	Scientist	Lab Assistant	Novice
3. Location & Access 3.1 Locate sources. 3.2 Find information within sources.	Gathers lab materials: independently; appropriately.	Gathers lab materials: with some assistance; appropriately.	Needs assistance: missing some materials.	Needs assistance: missing most materials.
4. Use of Information 4.1 Engage (e.g., read, hear, view). 4.2 Extract relevant information.	Journal includes daily entries; is appropriate to task; is accurate.	Journal includes almost daily entries; is appropriate to task; is accurate.	Journal includes some entries; is inappropriate to task; is accurate or inaccurate.	Journal includes few or no entries.
5. Synthesis 5.1 Organize information from multiple sources. 5.2 Present the result.	Lab write-up complete and has proper format. Logical conclusion based on results.	Lab write-up not complete or problems with format. Logical conclusion based on results.	Lab write-up okay. Conclusion needs work.	Problems with lab write-up and/or format. Conclusion needs work.

Figure D: Blank Big6 Scoring Guide

Worksheet 6-3—Big6™ Assessment Scoring Guide

Big6™ Skills Eisenberg/Berkowitz © 1988		Highly Competent 10 points		Competent 8 points		Adequate 7 points		Not Yet Acceptable 5 points	Evidence	Focus
1. Task Definition 1.1 Define the problem. 1.2 Identify the information needed.	S T L		S T L		S T L		S T L			
2. Information Seeking Strategies 2.1 Determine all possible sources. 2.2 Select the best source.	S T L		S T L		S T L		S T L			
3. Location & Access 3.1 Locate sources. 3.2 Find information within sources.	S T L		S T L		S T L		S T L			
4. Use of Information 4.1 Engage (e.g., read, hear, view). 4.2 Extract relevant information.	S T L		S T L		S T L		S T L			
5. Synthesis 5.1 Organize information from multiple sources. 5.2 Present the result.	S T L		S T L		S T L		S T L			
6. Evaluation 6.1 Judge the result (effectiveness). 6.2 Judge the process (efficiency).	S T L		S T L		S T L		S T L			

(S) Student, (T) Teacher, (L) Library Media Specialist

Figure D: Blank Big6 Scoring Guide

Worksheet 6-3—Big6™ Assessment Scoring Guide (cont.)

Big6™ Skills Eisenberg/Berkowitz © 1988		Highly Competent 10 points		Competent 8 points		Adequate 7 points		Not Yet Acceptable 5 points	Evidence	Focus
1. Task Definition 1.1 Define the problem. 1.2 Identify the information needed.	S T L		S T L		S T L		S T L			
2. Information Seeking Strategies 2.1 Determine all possible sources. 2.2 Select the best source.	S T L		S T L		S T L		S T L			
3. Location & Access 3.1 Locate sources. 3.2 Find information within sources.	S T L		S T L		S T L		S T L			
4. Use of Information 4.1 Engage (e.g., read, hear, view). 4.2 Extract relevant information.	S T L		S T L		S T L		S T L			
5. Synthesis 5.1 Organize information from multiple sources. 5.2 Present the result.	S T L		S T L		S T L		S T L			
6. Evaluation 6.1 Judge the result (effectiveness). 6.2 Judge the process (efficiency).	S T L		S T L		S T L		S T L			

(S) Student, (T) Teacher, (L) Library Media Specialist

Part VII: Partnerships and Collaboration

The Big6™ Partnerships and Collaboration

Introduction

In our society today — in business, public service, and education — no one works or succeeds in isolation. This is particularly true of Big6™ Skills instruction. Throughout this Handbook, in our other works, and in our workshops and presentations, we emphasize that effective Big6™ Skills instruction is accomplished within the context of subject area classroom learning.

We champion, promote, and work hard to facilitate an integrated, curriculum-based approach to skills development, and that requires true collaboration and partnership among classroom teachers, teacher-librarians, technology teachers, administrators, parents, community members, and students.

An integrated, collaborative approach is a departure from the traditional way that library, technology, and classroom teaching staff interact. In the past, school librarians would instruct students on library skills such as how to use dictionaries and encyclopedias or magazine indexes. This instruction was often done in isolation — far removed from the day-to-day activities of the classroom. More recently, we found computer teachers in computer labs teaching keyboarding, word processing, or information searching skills. Here too, the instruction was in isolation — without any connection to the subject content of classes.

Linking to Classroom Needs

Fortunately, these situations are changing. Teacher-librarians and computer teachers recognize that students learn better when instruction is linked to the needs of the classroom. We are seeing more and more partnerships among educators to design and implement learning situations in which skills and content are coordinated and integrated.

The material in this part of *The Definitive Big6™ Workshop Handbook* will assist you in understanding the importance of collaboration and will help you consider alternative approaches to forming partnerships within your schools and districts. The activity sheet and worksheets are designed to help make the Big6™-classroom connections. Bob's article from *School Library Media Activities Monthly* addresses collaboration head-on and Mike's article from *MultiMedia Schools* are calls-to-action to form meaningful information and technology teams in schools.

Overview

Information & Technology Skills for Student Success: The Big6™ Skills Approach

Implementation

- **Foundation:** the information problem-solving process (the Big6™)
- **Context:** real needs in real situations
  - school, life, work
  - assignments: papers, reports, projects
- **Approach:**
  - coordination ➛ cooperation ➛ collaboration
  - teachers, administrators, library media specialists, parents, community members
- **Partnership:**
  - School and Community Wide
  - Classroom teachers
  - Library and information specialists
  - Technology teachers
  - Administration and curriculum coordinators
  - Parents!

Worksheet 7-1—Information Base

Compare and contrast the knowledge, attitudes, and skills of teachers, school library media specialists, and technology specialists.

	Teachers	Library Media Specialists	Technology Specialists
Knowledge			
Attitudes			
Skills			

Activity Sheet

What attitudes and actions promote collaborative instructional planning? The next exercise will help analyze the Collaborative Instructional Activity Planning Process. Use the area below to take notes.

Developing Big6™ Understandings

Worksheet 7-2

Curriculum Context: Create a typical, integrated curriculum situation. Describe one or two activities that relate to each of the Big6™ Skills.

Big6™ Skills	Activities
1. Task Definition 1.1 Define the problem. 1.2 Identify the information needed.	
2. Information Seeking Strategies 2.1 Determine all possible sources. 2.2 Select the best source.	
3. Location & Access 3.1 Locate sources. 3.2 Find information within sources.	
4. Use of Information 4.1 Engage (e.g., read, hear, view). 4.2 Extract relevant information.	
5. Synthesis 5.1 Organize information from multiple sources. 5.2 Present the result.	
6. Evaluation 6.1 Judge the result (effectiveness). 6.2 Judge the process (efficiency).	

Worksheet 7-3: Instructional Strategies Development Sheet

List and describe alternative generic instructional strategies for each of the Big6™ Skills.

1. Task Definition

1.1 Define the task (the information problem).
1.2 Identify the information needed in order to complete the task (to solve the information problem).

2. Information Seeking Strategies

2.1 Determine the range of possible sources.
2.2 Evaluate the possible sources to determine priorities.

Worksheet 7-3: Instructional Strategies Development Sheet (cont.)

3. Location & Access

3.1 Locate sources (intellectually and physically).
3.2 Find information within sources.

4. Use of Information

4.1 Engage (e.g., read, hear, view) the information in a source.
4.2 Extract information from a source.

Worksheet 7-3: Instructional Strategies Development Sheet (cont.)

5. Synthesis

5.1 Organize information from multiple sources.
5.2 Present information.

6. Evaluation

6.1 Judge the product (effectiveness).
6.2 Judge the process (efficiency)

Worksheet 7-4 — Curriculum Situations & Big6™ Connection

Curriculum Situations	Big6™ Connection

Collaboration: Partnerships for Instructional Improvement

By Bob Berkowitz, with Max Steiner and John DonVito

[Editor's Note: The example used in this article is a collaborative unit developed for tenth graders. However, the unit may easily be modified for lower grade levels and, more importantly, it is only an example that is used to illustrate the collaborative process.]

The value of an integrated approach to library and information skills instruction in undeniable. It promotes cooperative planning between teachers and library media specialists, and commitment to joint goals and objectives. It is through the integrated instructional model that the content curriculum and library and information problem solving skills are linked to provide meaningful information skills instruction. However, in order to implement the integrated model effectively and gain maximum benefits, both teachers and library media specialists face two problems:

1. How to select the best opportunities within the content curriculum scope and sequence with which to integrate, and
2. How to design instructional units that motivate students to learn and use information problem-solving skills effectively.

Teachers are undoubtedly the best source of information regarding the taught curriculum—the content and structure, the scope and sequence of what really goes on in the classroom. Teachers are able to ensure that the content and timing of the instructional unit is appropriate and meets the needs of students. A library media specialist, acting in the instructional-consultant role, can ensure that the instructional unit integrates library and information skills in ways that are involving, challenging, and meaningful to students. Additionally, library media specialists can provide a school-wide perspective of the information skills that need to be taught or reviewed as necessary. Teachers and library media specialists, acting collaboratively, can explore a range of creative and logical learning experiences, and design instructional units that teach, remediate, or review content and information skills. Understanding the roles that both teachers and library media specialists play is only the first step to successful collaborative efforts. Ultimately, the willingness of teachers and library media specialists to involve themselves actively in the collaborative design of instruction units is essential to success. Initial success builds partners for continued collaborative efforts.

One such collaborative effort, "Renaissance to Industrialization: A Social, Political, and Economic Comparison," is a tenth grade Global Studies unit based on the Big Six Skills © (Eisenberg and Berkowitz, 1990) approach to information skills instruction, which meets the twofold challenge of timing and motivation. Our previous experiences at collaboration had focused on enhancing the quality of existing classroom activities and student achievement. By analyzing instruction, content, and student performance from an information problem-solving perspective, we redesigned the existing course content to incorporate information problem-solving skills. The results of this effort were that students were more confident in their ability to use content information to complete assignments. This was reflected both in the quality of the products and presentations as well as in test scores. We had realized our goals. Based on this success, we were eager to try our hand at designing an integrated unit that would extend our instructional program in Global Studies. We decided to try something not usually viewed as an obvious target to integration with library and information skills instruction, to develop a unit that would review and remediate content. The result is the unit described below, and included in this article.

"Renaissance to Industrialization: A Social, Political and Economic Comparison" is taught at the end of the first semester as an opportunity for students to review and relearn 350 years of history within a two-week period. The motivational strategy that we decided to use was to incorporate student interest in role-playing games and family history with small-group work and multiple presentation opportunities in order to have students use information in a variety of ways. Given this set of parameters, we took what we believe is an interesting (if not unique) approach. As you read through the unit, we hope it is obvious that it capitalizes on its ability to release students' imaginations. And, through its variety of presentation modes, it affords students multiple opportunities to exhibit this command of the content information.

For an information-skills perspective, the Big Six Skills © focus this unit is on Task Definition, Information Use, Synthesis, and Evaluation. Students are engaged in important skills activities, including:

- understanding and explaining the requirements of the assignment,
- determining the information needs,
- reading for content,
- selecting and summarizing useful information,
- organizing information for a variety of presentations,
- listening for a purpose, and
- assessing the presentations.

All these, of course, while students are reviewing and relearning the significant events, people, and concepts that comprise 350 years of history.

Some of the management and organizational keys that made this instructional unit successful for our students included:

- clearly defining our expectations to students,
- systematically breaking down tasks into manageable parts and monitoring students' work daily,
- carefully determining the student mix for each of the small groups, by considering learning styles, ability, personality,
- continually providing clear feedback and direction from the teacher, and

- enthusiastically encouraging students to engage history and explore "their" past.

Throughout the collaborative process, each of us was committed to creating an instructional unit in which students would have a successful experience, one characterized by cooperation, respect for each other' ideas and opinions, and a positive attitude to a new approach to teaching and learning social studies. We were pleased with students' eager participation and the quality of their presentations. Each member of each small group was able to contribute to the success of the entire group. The discussion of content took place as students helped each other review and relearn the historical facts and their implications. Students were involved in discussing history as cause and effect, and had a "personal" interest in how events, people, and concepts affected "their family." Other benefits included the chance to practice communication skills that resulted from the sharing among students groups and the opportunity for students to present their ideas orally and visually. All in all, we had improved the quality of the time students spent immersed in learning history.

We urge you to adopt (or adapt) this unit for use with your social studies teachers and students. It is easy to personalize this unit to fit your own situation. Although we used this particular unit with tenth grade, the idea is applicable to a range of grade levels. Additionally, it is possible to add to any of the activities by either extending the ones we have developed or by incorporating new activities, perhaps a student-designed timeline or a videotaped project. Another way to localize this unit is to adopt its basic instructional strategy and structure but change the time period, or region. For example, a similar unit might be designed around the time period from the Civil War to the Civil Rights Movement.

The benefit to students was great, and they are now eager to experiment with new ways of learning history and to participate in activities we are currently creating in new instructional units. The benefit for the three of us was equally great. We each have a renewed appreciation of the others' roles in the design and implementation of quality learning experiences for students.

Unit: Renaissance to Industrialization: A Social, Political, and Economic Comparison

Audience: Global Studies (Grade 10)

Overview: This unit of instruction gives students the opportunity to review 350 years of history from a variety of perspectives. Social, political, and economic changes that occurred in England from 1500 to 1850 are the focus. The device used to meet this goal and stimulate student interest is the concept of family history. Students, working cooperatively in small groups, are required to assume that they are people living in England in 1850. Their task is to create a "family tree" of direct descendents dating back to 1500. Additionally, students are required to write a short family history and present an oral portrait of two family members from each century. As part of the family history, students are required to incorporate two significant historical events or concepts, and two historical personalities, as well as comment on the impact of one social, one political, and one economic issue for each family member "portrait."

Rationale: It is important for students to be able to trace the changes in major historical themes (social, political, economic influences) as a means to understanding history. Additionally, this project acts as a review, remediation, and reinforcement exercise.

Subject Area Objectives: The major objectives to be covered in this unit of study include, but are not limited to:

Social: Students will demonstrate their understanding of:

- the movement of large portions of the population from farms to cities.
- how living and working conditions changed.
- the effect of religious intolerance and the impact of religious affiliation on daily life.
- the changes in culture (e.g., the ideas that characterized Renaissance thought).
- the distribution of wealth.
- the reasons for and effects of the Reformation.
- how Enlightenment's ideas spread throughout society.
- how socialists proposed to deal with changes in society.

Political: Students will demonstrate their understanding of:

- the change from absolute monarchy to limited monarchy to constitutional state.
- the causes and effects of revolutions.
- the impact of laws (e.g., Factory Act).
- imperialism.
- role of government and its impact on daily life.
- how disagreements between kings and Parliament led to civil war.
- the aftermath of the English Civil War.

Economic: Students will demonstrate their understanding of:

- the changes that occurred in the English economy in the 1500's and 1600's.
- the growth of socialism.
- the influence of the factory system.
- how mercantilism (trade with foreign countries) changed trade and business practices.
- the effect of unionism.
- changes in personal finances.
- how England took part in exploration and trade, and the role England played in the colonization of North America.
- how Queen Elizabeth I brought prosperity to England.
- why the Industrial Revolution began in Great Britain.
- how new inventions and methods of production helped to transform industry.

Big Six Objectives:

Task Definition: Students will demonstrate the ability to:
- explain the requirements of the assignment.
- create questions to research.

Information Use: Students will demonstrate the ability to:
- select appropriate information.
- acquire information from a variety of sources.
- summarize information.

Synthesis: Students will demonstrate the ability to:
- prepare a "family tree" (visual).
- prepare "family portraits" report (written).
- make class presentations (oral).

Evaluation: Students will demonstrate the ability to:
- assess products (visual, written, oral) based on the evaluation criteria.
- assess classmates' oral presentations based on criteria given.
- convey appropriate information accurately.
- convey accurate information appropriately.

Materials:

"Significant Events, Concepts, and People" Sheet
"Information about the Characters" Sheet
Examples of family trees
Examples of family histories / chronicles / diaries
"Audience Information Collection and Evaluation" Sheets
Peer Evaluation Sheets

Significant Events, Concepts, and People

1500s (Examples)

Sea Dogs	Phillip II of Spain
Act of Supremacy	Henry VIII
Raleigh settles Roanoke	Harvey
Elizabeth becomes Queen	Thomas More
Bloody Mary is Queen	Sir Francis Drake
War of Roses	John Hawkins
Spanish Armada	Henry VII
Guilds	Jane Seymour
Plague	Prince Edward
Elizabeth I	

1600s (Examples)

Puritan Revolution	Shakespeare
Glorious Revolution	Cromwell
Etc.	

1700s (Examples)

American Revolution	George III
Prime Minister	Walpole
Etc.	

1800s (Example)

Act of Union	Tennyson
Urbanization	Keats
Etc.	

Information about the Characters

General Knowledge: As you read about the characters in this role-playing simulation, it is important to know that one characteristic that each of these people have in common is that from one generation to the next, the family occupation has generally remained similar. In those instances in which occupations did change, the change was as the result of social, political, or economic facts that impacted the family. If that occurred within the family history of your character, you will need to indicate the event or situation that accounts for the change in occupation.

Curator of Westminster Abbey and Windsor Castle
Edmond Crenshire is a member of the wealthy class. He maintains church records and art treasures of the realm. He is directly responsible to the Archbishop of Canterbury. Edmond Crenshire is a crotchety old geezer who hates change. He has been the Curator for more than 40 years. He is interested in the arts and especially literature. He meets regularly with representatives of the Archbishop. Edmond is keenly aware of the power of the written word. He was a regular visitor at the court of King George III.

Factory Worker
Lydia's grandmother and grandfather lived on a farm in rural Yorkshire. Now, however, she is working in a factory in Leeds. She is concerned about her family and unionism. Lydia is 37 years old. She lives with her husband who is also a factory worker and their six children, ages three to fourteen. One of her children, a daughter age ten, died two years ago in a factory accident.

Factory Owner
Arthur Newbury is owner of a textile factory that makes cotton yard goods. He is concerned about overseas trace, decreasing profits, and the growth of socialism. A member of a men's club, he is adamant in his opposition to government interference and, for that matter, any laws that will give workers rights. He is in favor of a laissez-faire approach to government. He lives with his wife and four children in Manchester.

Scientist/Inventor
Jonathan Smyth is a free-thinking individual whose background is blacksmithing and tinsmithing. Lately, he has been experimenting with something he calls the "puddling process." He is a friend of Mr. Bessimer. Mr. Smyth, who is only 36 years old, is not married, and can devote much of his time to designing machine parts for factory equipment and creating new types of machinery to increase textile production.

Member of the House of Lords
Sir Reginald Appleton's main concern is maintaining the power of the wealthy and nobility. He is a member of the Anglican Church. Sir Reginald's family has held a seat in the House of Lords since the 1300s. He lives in a manor house in Lands End with his wife, five children (four daughters and a son age 12), and a number of servants.

Member of the House of Commons
James Tewkson is a Puritan. James is concerned about the working conditions in factories. Additionally, he is concerned with other social issues such as health and morality. He was elected by the people of Kent, a Borough outside of London James. Like his father before him, he is a barrister of some financial means.

Merchant
Charles Crawford owns a women's clothing store in Manchester. His primary customers are wealthy women. His store is a center for gossip among wealthy women. Keeping his ear open to his customers' conversations for more than their fashion likes and dislikes, he also can keep tabs on the latest political and economic issues of the day. Charles invests his considerable profits in overseas trading.

Naval Officer
Richard Seaforth is a captain in the Royal Navy. His present commission is as Captain of the Frigate Rockingham. Richard's father was also a navy man. When Richard was seven years old, his father was able to get his son a situation as a cabinboy. The Seaforth family lives in Liverpool. Richard spends from eight-ten months at a time at sea. He is well read, and spends much of his time reading the history of great naval battles. Richard once met men who served on the frigate Macedonian. Captain Seaforth is anxious to transfer to an expeditionary force.

Information Use Plan for "Family Portrait"		
Date	**Events/Concepts**	**People**
Social		
Political		
Economic		
As a group, research all of the events/concepts and choose which ones to include in each written portrait. Use the "Impact" sheet to record your information.		

Impact of Events/Concepts and People x Century

Event:

____

____

____

Concept:

____

____

____

Person:

____

____

____

Audience Information Collection and Evaluation Sheet

Other than your own group, which group made the most accurate presentation of the social, political, and economic changes which occured from 1500-1850? Explain your decision.

Activities:

1. Introduction to the project and its requirements. Students will be divided into small groups and assigned "characters." Each group will research events / concepts and people (see list).
2. Teacher will define "family tree" as a graphic representation that shows relationships among family members in and across generations. Students will be shown sample "family trees" and directed in a brainstorming session to determine creative and alternative ways of graphically representing family history.
3. Working in small groups, students will begin to develop their "family trees."
4. Students will begin the process of researching the background of each family member about whom they choose to write. Students will complete the "family portrait by person" plan.
5. Teachers will review the requirements for the written "family portrait" / biography. Students continue to meet in small groups (and work individually) to develop their "family history," design their graphic presentation, and continue their research.
6. Students display "family trees."
7. Students present oral report (20 minutes for each group including question-and-answer period). Students in audience complete "audience information collection and evaluation" sheet.
8. Students submit all written work as well as graphic representation.

Evaluation:

General Guidelines: Students will receive group grades. Each group will be graded based on the following criteria:

Completeness of Plan—20%

- including: the required amount of information, its accuracy and appropriateness

Oral Presentation—20%

- including: accuracy, appropriateness and completeness of the information

Evaluation—20%

- based on: peer evaluation comments

Family Tree and Written Report—40%

- based on: completeness, accuracy in the use of appropriate information.

Peer Evaluation Sheet				
		Events/ Concepts	**People**	Explain why you think the character was/ wasn't consistent with the times.
Character	**Social**	1 2 Impact	1 2 Impact	
Date	**Political**	1 2 Impact	1 2 Impact	
Person	**Economic**	1 2 Impact	1 2 Impact	

This article is reprinted with publisher's permission.

Berkowitz, R. E., Stoner, M., & DonVito, J. (1994). Collaboration: Partnerships for instructional improvement. *School Library Media Activities Monthly, 10*(7), 32-35.

Apply Big6™ Skills to Integrate Content Standards in the Curriculum

By Janet Murray

Increasingly, school districts are aligning the Big6 Skills with their state standards documents. The resulting charts and diagrams aligning standards with the Big6 Skills are helpful in designing integrated information literacy curricula. Potentially even more powerful, the alignments help classroom teachers and teacher-librarians to appreciate and understand how to use the Big6 to help their students achieve standards.

In this column, we will examine three different efforts that build on aligning the Big6 to standards.

Connecticut

In West Hartford, Connecticut, "all eighth grade students participate in the information and technology literacy course, which is part of the thirty-day unified arts rotation. This course completes the sequence that begins in sixth grade with thinking skills and continues in seventh grade with research strategies. Through this assured learning experience students will become efficient and effective users and producers of information, using the information and technology tools necessary for success in lifelong learning. ["Information and Technology Literacy Curriculum: Grade 8." 2002. West Hartford Public Schools. http://www.whps.org/library/ITL_Curriculum_Grade_8.htm]

Appendices align Big6 Skills with Connecticut's Learning Resources and Information Technology (LRIT) Content Standards as well as their Computer Technology Content Standards (which precisely mirror the National Educational Technology Standards for Students, NETS-S.)

New York

Clarkstown Central School District (West Nyack, NY) adopted a standards-based curriculum incorporating the Big6 Skills.

"With information literacy skills, students will possess the capability to transfer their information knowledge to real-life information needs situations. With this curriculum, students will master the use of information, whether that information is obtained from a library or on a home computer. The intent of Clarkstown's library curriculum framework is to create consistency and momentum in the district's information literacy program. This intent is directing our plan to fully integrate information literacy curriculum into the subject curriculum district-wide." ["Philosophy." Information Literacy Curriculum. 14 Sep. 2001 (http://www.ccsd.edu/bardonia/CCSDLibraryCurriculum/)]

Clarkstown aligned the National Information Literacy Standards (ALA) with New York State Learning Standards in a wide variety of subjects and developed performance indicators and benchmarks.

Minnesota

The Mankato Information and Technology Literacy Curriculum developed by a committee led by Doug Johnson provides the foundation for many similar efforts across the nation. "The information skills curriculum is centered around large projects at each grade level during each school year. These projects:

- use a version of the Big6 (© Eisenberg and Berkowitz) information processing model,
- have clearly stated objectives from I.S.D. 77 Information Skills curriculum, which in turn supports the State Graduation Rule requirements,
- are assessed in a complete and objective manner,
- use technologies and identified productivity software,
- build cumulatively on skills learned the previous year,
- and meet district benchmarks for each grade level, K-12.

http://www.isd77.k12.mn.us/resources/infocurr/infolit.html
The benchmarks refer to state standards in speaking, writing, inquiry and math.

Unique Features

Course Description

West Hartford's Information and Technology Literacy curriculum includes the course description and content, an invaluable guide to middle school teachers seeking a fully articulated plan. Students "create a WebQuest connected to a topic from one of the middle school curriculum areas" using the Big6 Skills and Connecticut standards as a framework. Goals, objectives, and content are all specified, with links to appropriate resources.

Appendices include web sites (with corresponding standards and grade levels) devoted to copyright, developing essential questions, Boolean logic, assessment, and graphic organizers (for teachers) and research guides, bibliography compilation and search skills for students. There is a template to organize the collection of bibliographic information, a rubric and self-reflection form to apply to the Big6 Skills (adapted from Teaching Technology and Information Skills: The Big6 in Secondary Schools), and a web site evaluation form. The glossary would be particularly helpful to those who may be unfamiliar with some of the vocabulary.

Scope and Sequence

The Clarkstown site includes a detailed list of grade level goals for each of the Big6 Skills that indicates at which grade each skill should be introduced, practiced and mastered. Another page identifies benchmarks at Grades 5, 8 and 12 for each of the information literacy indicators. This type of extensive detail can be helpful to library media specialists and teachers who grasp the concepts of the Big6 Skills and information literacy standards, but are unsure how to apply them in their own teaching situations.

The Clarkstown site also features more extensive alignment with subject area New York State Learning Standards than other sites that restrict their focus to information and technology literacy standards.

Benchmarks

Mankato identifies specific objectives for each of the "Little Twelve" and delineates benchmarks for each grade level, K-12, phrased as "I" statements in each of the following areas: Research and Inquiry Skills, Life-long Reading, Technology Skills, and Appropriate Use of Resources. The Mankato curriculum includes an additional goal framed in terms of the information-based economy for which we are preparing our students: "Potential employers of Mankato public school graduates should be confident that their new employees will know how to identify information needs, locate relevant information in an efficient manner, understand and evaluate information, and use the information to solve a problem, complete a task, or be able to communicate that information clearly to others. Graduates will be able to use technology effectively in the information problem solving process."

Where the Rubber Meets the Road

So, how can you actually use these resources to improve your students' acquisition and mastery of standards? As Ferdi would say, "This is where the rubber meets the road." These are my ideas:

Imagine you are a library media specialist collaborating with a middle school science teacher working on a unit on biomes. I would use the Clarkstown site to help identify connections between information literacy standards and New York learning standards in science <http://www.ccsd.edu/bardonia/CCSDLibraryCurriculum/CurriculumCommittee/standard.htm>. For example, "Learning Standards for Mathematics, Science, and Technology Standard 7 [states that] Students will apply the knowledge and thinking skills of mathematics, science, and technology to address real-life problems and make informed decisions." Does your state have a similarly worded standard in science?

The preservation of biomes is certainly a real-life issue. What a great opportunity to introduce critical thinking skills and information problem solving based on the Big6 Skills. West Hartford's curriculum defines a student-created WebQuest as the final product. Good WebQuests incorporate roles that require multiple perspectives and require higher level thinking to construct new meaning. If your students aren't ready to create their own, consider using one or more of those listed on Tom March's new site, Best WebQuests.com, or apply his rubric to others you find. <http://bestwebquests.com/bwq/matrix.asp>

The Clarkstown site associates the following middle school grade level goals with the Big6 Skills (as I think they apply to this assignment):

- Task Definition: Create specific questions and use them to develop a thesis statement or hypothesis (P)
- Information Seeking Strategies: Determine what information is relevant (P)
- Location and Access: Analyze the timeliness, authoritativeness and reliability of the information (P)
- Use of Information: Read, view or listen for major ideas and keywords to identify relevant information from a variety of sources (P)

- Synthesis: Appraise the information gathered to see if it solves the information problem (I/P) and Make and support personal assertions (I/P)
- Evaluation: Inquiry Process: Scope of inquiry was relevant and authentic (P)

Use the web site resources listed in West Hartford's curriculum to help students develop essential questions and evaluate the web sites they plan to use. Use the Mankato objectives and benchmarks to help teachers focus their research assignments on standards and information problem solving. Use the templates from the Minnesota "Electronic Curriculum Repository" to guide the development of lessons or units integrating research skills and content standards.

Compare to Other States

Three of the states whose standards were featured in the previous column (Fall 2002 Vol. E-3 No. 2 http://fp3e.adhost.com/big6/enewsletter/murray.shtml) also have useful resources to consult.

North Carolina's "Resources" page lists websites for lesson plans, assessment (rubrics), web resources and activities. [http://www.ncpublicschools.org/curriculum/Information/resources.html]

The Washington Library Media Association lists information literacy benchmarks aligned with each of the Big6 Skills for grades 4, 7 and 10. [http://www.wlma.org/Instruction/benchmarks.htm]

Missouri's "Information and Technology Literacy Companion to the Show-Me Standards" includes a section of "sample learning activities that may be used to teach the various knowledge and performance skills" and emphasizes that "Many of the learning activities lend themselves to a cooperative instructional partnership between the teacher and the library media specialist." [http://www.dese.state.mo.us/divimprove/curriculum/literacy/]

Reprinted with permission. Murray, J. "Apply Big6™ Skills to Integrate Content Standards in the Curriculum." Big6 eNewsletter, Volume E4, Issue 1. Available online: http://www.big6.com/showenewsarticle.php?id=325

Call to Action: Getting Serious About Libraries and Information in Education

By Mike Eisenberg, Director, University of Washington School of Library and Information Science, and Carrie Lowe, Senior Education Associate, Education and Online Communication, Public Broadcasting System (PBS)

MultiMedia Schools March/April 1999

[Editor's Note: You may remember from your schooling the image of the FireTriangle. Fire can be sustained only when there is fuel, oxygen, and heat. As you'll see below, achieving technology's potential for learning requires a similar set of conditions. Evaluated, organized content is the fuel (provided by library media specialists); carefully planned instructional experiences is the oxygen (provided by classroom teachers); the commitment and energy to make things happen is the heat (provided by administrators). Firefighters know that all it takes to extinguish a fire is to break the link between any of these three elements. We need to be fire builders who can spark the flame of lifelong learning, and the following feature challenges us to begin.]

The work of the Information & Technology team goes beyond creating technology-rich learning environment for students, …

The Information & Technology Team

In the past few years, we've had the opportunity to work with educators and communities across the United States and all over the world. In that time, we've seen some highly effective information and technology programs, and others that are, uh, frankly less than effective. Why do some schools and districts thrive in terms of meaningful integration of technology with learning and teaching while others do not?

This, of course, is a complicated question. There are many factors that contribute to the successful use of technology in education, including:

- vision and clear setting of goals and objectives
- training and continuous support for teachers
- systematic and continuous planning, evaluation, and revision

However, in our experience, there is one aspect of successful technology deployment that is even more important than all of these together—teamwork. We're not talking about a general, pollyanna-ish, "let's all work together" approach to teamwork. We are talking about a true integration of information, library, and instructional technology services, systems, resources, and roles in a unified Information & Technology team.

The members of the Information & Technology team can be found within your own school: technology teachers, library and information professionals, and key administrators. All you need to add is commitment, enthusiasm, and teamwork. A unified I&T team is one in which team members work together to provide services and resources to classroom teachers, students, and even parents. Schools with strong, committed I&T teams invariably see great results in their schools, and not only in terms of what their students are learning. These collaborative programs enjoy excellent funding, the respect of their colleagues, and influence over administrative decisions.

The work of the Information & Technology team goes beyond creating a technology-rich learning environment for students, although this is one of their most important tasks. Great I&T teams have a close relationship with classroom teachers and administration, and their responsibilities affect every aspect of the school. They provide a technical support system by coordinating tech services and resources and coordinating purchasing decisions. In terms of curriculum, the I&T team oversees the information and technology literacy program and ensures that it is implemented as part of the classroom curriculum. An active, dynamic Information & Technology team is an integral part of the school; the team is the right arm of overburdened administrators and teachers.

Unfortunately, at this time, we don't see enough of these I&T teams in schools and districts. Too often we see library media specialists, technology teachers, and administrators working in isolation and fighting for turf and control. At the same time, these educators bemoan their feelings of professional disenfranchisement, their inability to interest colleagues in collaboration, being overwhelmed with just too much to do, and worst of all, budget cuts and eliminated positions. Although they all say that they are working toward a common goal—preparing students for success in the information age—they are not working together.

Is it possible for library media specialists and technology teachers to work together with administrators and other educators? It is not simply possible, it is necessary that they do so in order to become the active players in curriculum and instruction that they must be in the coming decades to ensure the success of students in the information age.

The Technology Question

The 1957 Katherine Hepburn and Spencer Tracy movie *Desk Set* tells the story of several librarians working in the research department of a newspaper whose jobs are threatened by the arrival of a computer designed to do their jobs better and faster. This suspicion of technology has not changed in the last 40 years; indeed, many of us, both teachers and library media specialists, dread the day that we are replaced by computers.

This is far from an irrational fear. For many of us, our first introduction to the idea of computers in the classroom came the day machines were wheeled into our classroom and dumped in the corner. This is a blatant intrusion onto our turf. We hear of other jobs, such as those in manufacturing, being replaced more and more by computers. Who hasn't looked in the corner of the classroom and imagined the computers there one day sitting on top of the desk you currently occupy at the front of the room, conducting the class?

Can library media specialists, technology teachers, and classroom teachers be replaced by technology? Absolutely not. We believe just the opposite. Library and information technology professionals are the true innovators of using technology to facilitate learning. As technology becomes more prevalent in learning and teaching, there is even greater need for information, library, and technology work in schools. This is a role that librarians can and must assume to create information-literate students.

The word "disintermediation" is batted around quite a bit in reference to future technologies. Disintermediation is the idea that as technology becomes more advanced, users will no longer require assistance to use it. The development of the World Wide Web has told a very different story. We have seen a staggering rise in the use of question-and-answer services (such as AskERIC, the question-and-answer service for education) in the past five years. As the Web becomes larger and more tangled, users need help finding what they want. This is where information and technology specialists step in.

The Key Is Teamwork

While our skills and strengths make us, as members of the Information & Technology team, the logical choice to lead students, teachers, and administrators into the information age, we cannot expect to have leadership roles handed to us. In order to take advantage of the opportunities awaiting us, it is necessary for us to reinvent ourselves. We cannot just expect to give our students more of the same in the next years; the changes in store for teaching and learning promise to be too profound.

We must reinvent ourselves as a dynamic, flexible team. It is impossible for any one of us—teachers and administrators, library media specialists, or technology teachers—to handle every responsibility the school of the future will present. To create the technology-rich learning center of the future, we need full partnership and true integration of responsibilities. By joining forces, we can share our strengths and assume a leadership role in schools and districts feeling the pressures of technology.

Facing the Challenge

No one is really sure what the school of the future will look like. We do know that it is going to be different, and a lot of that difference is going to be due to the influx of technology into classrooms and learning centers. This uncertainty means that library media specialists, technology teachers, and administrators must work together to answer three key questions: What needs to be done? Who will do it? Finally, how will it be done? These are the questions addressed here.

What Needs to be Done?

This question is deceptively simple. The first answer that comes to mind is "to integrate technology into learning and teaching." However, this is tantamount to not seeing the forest for the proverbial trees. It is key to remember why parents, school boards, and politicians are supplying us with computers for our schools and demanding that we use them.

The reason is, of course, that we are preparing students for a future that is very different from the one we faced as graduates. Even lower-level employment will demand familiarity and the ability to work with technology. For this reason, it is essential that we give students the tools and skills which will allow them to be successful in tomorrow's workplace.

What needs to be done goes beyond sitting students in front of a computer and showing them how to turn on the machine. We must work together with our colleagues to prepare students for the technology-rich workplace they will face in the future.

How Will It Be Done?

When strategizing with other educators about how to best prepare students, it is imperative to remember that we are preparing students for the technologies of tomorrow, not those of today. This means that we must teach students strategies and ways of thinking about technology, rather than discrete skill sets. After all, skills become obsolete when the technology they relate to becomes obsolete.

The key to equipping students with the skills that they will need to succeed in the future lies in information and technology literacy instruction. The new standard for library media programs, *Information Power*, defines information literacy as "the ability to find and use information" (AASL/AECT, p. 1). It goes on to say, "Students must become skillful consumers and producers of information in a range of sources and formats to thrive personally and economically in the information age" (p. 2). To create information-literate students, educators must concentrate on processes (such as information problem-solving and critical-thinking skills) rather than computer skills.

Students must be taught that technology is a tool rather than an answer in and of itself. Teach students that there are three uses of technology in a modern society—information technology (such as electronic resources), communication technology (telecommunications), and processing technology (software that helps us do better, faster work). Once students recognize that technology is a means to an end, they will be well on their way to being information-literate, productive citizens of a future society.

We teach technology skills within the overall information problem-solving process using the Eisenberg and Berkowitz Big6™ Skills approach (see the Big6™ Web site <http://big6.com>). The Big6™ is a tried and proven method of teaching information and technology skills in context (see Eisenberg and Johnson, 1996). The Big6™ can be considered from a number of perspectives — as an information and technology literacy curriculum, an information problem-solving process, a set of skills for effectively and efficiently meeting information needs, and an overall method for developing programs to help students learn essential information and technology skills.

Who Will Do It?

Preparing students for a technology-rich society that is unlike anything we have ever known is a tall order. It requires leadership, imagination, and hard work. To fulfill this mission, we need the skills and talents of all three members of the Information & Technology team: the technology teacher to implement and support instructional technology, the library media specialist to work with teachers to create information- and technology-rich curriculum, and the administrator to follow through and put plans into action.

However, the Information & Technology team cannot work alone. Team members must be sure that they are constantly communicating with classroom teachers, administrators, and school policy-makers to ensure that they are doing their jobs. If others are not included in important decisions to some extent, it is less likely that they will buy into resulting change.

At this point, we must proudly admit our biases. As librarians, we think that it is impossible to successfully prepare students for the information age without the help of the library and information professional. The skill of the librarian lies in finding exactly what is needed in a glut of information. This ability to look critically at information is an essential component of information and technology literacy.

The library and information professional brings the "information" component to the Information & Technology team. Information is a librarian's business, and librarians are most qualified to create and assist teachers in implementing information literacy instruction. In terms of technology, librarians have led the way in teaching students technology skills in context throughout their professional history.

Clearly, the library and information professional are essential components of the Information & Technology team. At the same time, we must stress the necessity for librarians to reinvent themselves as they face new professional challenges. It is key that every library media specialist who is serious about preparing students for the information age read *Information Power* and follow its directives for becoming dynamic, active information professionals.

[Editor's Note: I've found the Big6™ Newsletter to be an invaluable resource for visions, strategies, and tools to teach essential skills for the information age. See <http://www.big6.com/newsletter/index.html>.]

A "Call to Action"

Gary Hartzell, former school administrator, prolific author, and professor of education at the University of Nebraska, spoke recently at the Washington Library Media Association Conference. In his presentation, Hartzell pointed out that no course in any major school of education in this country focuses on the use of library and information in learning and teaching. He went on to say that in almost all teacher training programs, there is little mention of the role of the library media program and the library and information professional at all. You can be sure that the Information & Technology team suffers from the same lack of recognition.

Therefore, we end this article with a "call to action." It's similar to the one that we sent to LM_NET, the library media mailing list. What if… we all pledged to actively spread the word about the importance of information, libraries, and technology in learning and teaching? We know that everyone is busy and can't even keep up. But what if we did this anyway?

What if each of us dedicated ourselves to communicating to a wide audience the importance of information, libraries, and technology in learning and teaching? *Information Power* states that our mission is "to ensure that students and staff are effective users of ideas and information." Isn't it time we explained what this really means and how we must work together to make it so?

One clear way is for library and information professionals, technology teachers, and administrators to market themselves as the Information & Technology team. This message must be directed at schools of education and teacher training programs. This is a task we must undertake for the future of learning and teaching. We must get in touch with the local university and volunteer to speak in teacher training classes. We must lobby for a course on information, information literacy, and information technology (or volunteer to teach it ourselves). If new teachers and administrators have no training in use of libraries and information in their schools, how can we expect them to change? This is our first (and perhaps most important) task as the Information & Technology team of tomorrow.

References

American Association of School Librarians and Association for Educational Communications and Technology (1998). *Information Power: Building Partnerships for Learning.* Chicago: American Library Association.

Eisenberg, M. and Berkowitz, R. (1998) "The Big6™ Skills," <http://big6.com>.

Eisenberg, M. and Johnson, D. (1996). "Computer Skills for Information Problem-Solving: Learning and Teaching Technology in Context," ERIC Digest. Syracuse, NY: ERIC Clearinghouse on Information & Technology. Available online at <http://ericir.syr.edu/ithome/digests/computerskills.html>.

Communications to the authors may be directed to:

Dr. Michael B. Eisenberg, Director, University of Washington School of Library and Information Science, Box 352930, Seattle, WA 98195-2930; 206/543-1794; e-mail: mbe@u.washington.edu

Carrie Lowe, 534 E. Nelson Ave., Alexandria, VA 22031, e-mail: carrie_a_lowe@yahoo.com

This article is reprinted with the author's permission.

Eisenberg, M.E., and Lowe, C. (1999). Call to action: Getting serious about libraries and information education. *MultiMedia Schools,* 6 (2), 18–21.

Moving Every Child Ahead: The Big6™ Success Strategy

By Bob Berkowitz, Library Media Specialist, Wayne Central School, Ontario Center, New York, with Ferdi Serim, *MultiMedia Schools* Editor

MultiMedia Schools, May/June 2002

Leaving No Child Behind: High-Stakes Testing as Information Problem Solving

In far too many schools, the prospect of annual testing for all students in grades 3–8 has needlessly paralyzed progress toward education reform and technology integration. As schools circle the wagons to meet the challenge of high-stakes tests, fear-based responses often sacrifice the higher-order-thinking, project-based-learning approaches, upon which successful uses of technology depend, in favor of rote learning. Our cover story features a proven strategy, which instead *improves performance by improving thinking* on the part of teachers and students alike. The powerful partnership of Bob Berkowitz and Scott Hopsicker, using the Big6™ process, gives us a working model for seizing this opportunity to advance effective teaching and learning by treating the tests themselves as information-based problems.

The Big6™ is the most widely known and used approach to teaching information and technology skills in the world. Used in thousands of K–12 schools, higher-education institutions, and corporate adult training programs, the Big6™ information problem-solving model is applicable whenever people need and use information. The Big6™ integrates information search and use skills along with technology tools in a systematic process to find, use, apply, and evaluate information to specific needs and tasks. Mike Eisenberg, co-creator of the Big6™ along with Bob Berkowitz, says, "Our mission is to help all people succeed by becoming better information problem-solvers. We live in an increasingly complex information- and technology-rich world. Information and technology skills are the 'new basics.' Being able to find and use information more effectively is essential to the success of students of all ages—pre-K through adult."

As this is the most vital issue facing our profession, I encourage you to share this story with your administrators, your school board, your community, and your peers. Together, we can work our way beyond teaching to the test, to the higher ground of improved learning for all.

—Ferdi Serim

An All-Too-Common Problem

Scott Hopsicker was a social studies teacher at Wayne Central High School, near Rochester, New York, when he first came to see me in 1997–1998. Even though he'd been at Wayne Central for only two years, Scott was a very active and popular teacher. He was involved in coaching as well as teaching and was well liked by his students. But he had a problem. In his first year as a teacher, Scott's students did not perform well on the New York State Regents Exam in American History. Remembering that first year, Scott says, "Only 53% passed, and I was horrified. I looked at myself first. I didn't blame the kids. I went to Bob soon afterwards."

Concerned about his students, and wanting to do something to help them improve their scores, Scott spoke to our assistant principal, who suggested that he discuss the situation with me, in my role as the school's library media specialist. Since I'd succeeded in helping students on advanced placement tests in various subjects, perhaps I could help. Scott saw himself as a conscientious, well-prepared teacher. He obviously needed a new strategy. Enter the Big6™.

First thing, when Scott came by and dropped off a couple of binders, I said, "I can tell you right now—you probably taught every small fact, being a first-year teacher, and you didn't actually teach concepts or themes." He was more of an instructor than a teacher. Scott recalls, "I presented information and then expected the students to keep up to date on it—I was assuming things."

Eyes on the Prize

What motivates teachers? Student performance! But this involves far more than test scores, far more than "covering the content." The test is nothing more than an interim objective to a greater goal: moving students from teacher-dependent to independent and lifelong learners. People often focus on what they want kids to know and be able to do. We add to this how we want them to be: capable, confident, independent learners.

We wanted to turn the exam experience into the basis for a powerful learning experience. To do this, you have to know: Which race are you running? Which skills are you practicing? If you are in the hurdles, and all you do is practice running, never practicing jumping, on the day of the race, you're going to be in for a sad surprise! So we had to analyze all the skills required and match these up with the processes and how the content would be used to gain these skills.

The Big6™: An Umbrella Strategy

The Big6™ approach to information-based problem solving provided Scott and me with the tools we needed to reinvent his teaching. This may sound bold, but anything less would not have done the job. Working as his coach and mentor throughout the year, we treated instructional design as a series of information-based problems or decisions. This allowed Scott to change his style of teaching from a content-driven approach to a Big6™ information-process-driven approach. The payoff was huge. After one year, his students went from a 53% passing rate to 91%. The next year the rate rose to 99%, with 75% of the students attaining mastery level. The third year (and beyond) has continued this pattern of success.

Such success required time and effort. For the entire year, I spent two hours each week with Scott, along with an additional two hours of follow-up on my own as I did my "information professional" homework. Scott spent six hours per week of his prep time — at least two of his three prep periods based on a four-day rotation — doing his homework. Then Scott had me come in and observe his teaching, so I could see his styles and strengths as well as some of his weaknesses. I also wanted to see the kids in action and how they reacted to Scott. Then we came up with activities and projects. He would tell me what content things he wanted them to know. I helped Scott decide what we wanted to base the projects on, and how often. *[Editor's note: These experiences form the basis of a new series of Big6™ workshops and conference presentations designed to expand the reach of what's been learned. See <http://www.big6.com>.]*

Scott Hopsicker is quite direct and unapologetic. "My goal is to make my students successful on the test. Yes, we use Regents essays and questions, but we really don't water down the curriculum. We did projects in addition to the essay preparation and test-taking work. We created cause-and-effect projects so the students can see how everything is connected together, not just little pieces and fragments. History is all one piece — all one smooth flow. It's kind of like reading a book from start to finish; everything is connected somehow."

Instructional Design: A Series of Information-Based Decisions

We knew that to move from a content-driven to an information-process-driven basis of instruction, we needed to learn more about the characteristics of high-quality instruction, which include the following:

- Higher-order thinking skills
- Repetition of good practices
- Moving from teacher-dependent to independent student learning behaviors
- Levels of learning: literal, interpretive, applied

Unlike other information problem solving strategies, the Big6™ is both diagnostic and prescriptive. This is the key difference, an empowering difference, to the Big6™ approach. We look at the process, as well as student performance, all along the way. We get rid of ineffective practices that are dragging us down. We not only see what's working (and what needs to work better), but we and our students see how to change, to bring us to our goal.

For example, in a content-driven model, we focus on standards, on what is taught (teacher behavior). However, we don't focus as much on what is learned (student behavior) until the test, when it is often too late. Moving from high-stakes tests to higher-order thinking requires a different framework for instruction. Providing the tools and skills to build meaning gives them the foundation they need for understanding, not just regurgitation of short-term factoids.

Scott Hopsicker's Study Tips

© Berkowitz & Hopsicker, 1998

1. **Time Management:**
   - How much time do you spend studying?
   - How much of the time is quality time?
   - Is the time quiet, free from distractions?
   - How much time is spent searching for information?

2. **Extra Help:**
   - Do I need to get help from my teacher?
   - I can meet with Mr. Hopsicker before homeroom (starting at 6:30 a.m.), during homeroom, during his open periods, for lunch, or after school.
   - Please just make an appointment

3. **Learning Strategies:**
   - Rewrite notes/review sheets
   - Redo chapter worksheets
   - Make flash cards: person/term/or event on one side; information on other side of the card: cause/effect/impact/contribution/ positive/negative
   - Note blanks: Cover up information in your notes, then write in missing gap
   - Use a tape recorder: Talk into a tape recorder using information, or without information
   - Read chapter and take notes on most important information
   - Review with family member, friend, or classmate
   - Use a combination of techniques listed from above
   - Use any other learning strategy that enables you to achieve your best score

Formula for Success: E1 + E2 = E3

Engage (read) +
Extract (notes, talk about it, chart) =
Ensure (result = better grades)

Discourse: Missing Links to Learning

Teachers don't think like information professionals. They don't ever ask, "How is information in this content area organized?" Scott and I approached history as "SPEFA," the interplay of social, political, economic, and foreign affairs events. We did exercises and projects that reinforced cause-and-effect relationships. So in learning geography, the impact of a river as a barrier to trade (or an aid to trade), or the different responses to various technologies in different cultures allowed students to exercise their minds, not just their memories. Now I've given them coat hangers, a place to put information, instead of just throwing it into their mental closets. If I present information as random dots and ask students to exactly recreate the pattern, there's no way that will happen. If instead I draw lines connecting the dots, creating a graphic, showing them the underlying structure of the information, they now have the tools to function at a higher level. Their learning becomes deeper and more lasting, as we know from 30 years of cognitive science.

Scott Hopsicker notes, "What I like about the Big6™ is that you assume nothing and that it's really common sense. You just apply the common sense you use in everyday life to school things."

We were surprised to learn that vocabulary needs went beyond the content we wanted to teach. Vocabulary within the instructions was a significant barrier for many students, particularly at-risk kids without a history of success and confidence. Students can be thrown off and perform at levels far below their capabilities and preparation simply by not grasping what they're being asked to do. Scott says, "We focus on difficult vocabulary words in the essay instructions. Instructions such as 'identify and discuss' are different than 'compare and contrast.' Even in high school, students still won't know what those words mean. We quiz them on the words and continually reinforce their correct use."

We used the information we gathered on a daily basis, both in terms of what was being taught, and the feedback we got from student performance. One key strategy we used was having daily quizzes…success breeds success and "points are cheap." Another key strategy was involving parents as part of the solution. (See the sidebars "Scott Hopsicker's Study Tips" and "Helping With Homework: A Big6™ Assignment Organizer.")

Scott notes another key student need. "One of the problems students in high school have is writing essays. So we created a new essay strategy for them—how to find, organize, and present information for essays. We used something called the "perfect chart" (see the sidebar "Perfect Chart: Cases and Issues"), which helps the students outline the essay first. The students develop charts, and I develop one, too. My chart is the "perfect" one—it includes all the information needed to get a perfect 100 score on the essay. So, there is no guessing game. The students know exactly what it takes to get a 100."

Another surprise was the balance of content and process. Scott remembers, "I had someone from another school take a look at our essays strategy. She

Helping with Homework: A Big6™ Assignment Organizer

Assignment ______________________ **Due Date** ______________________

Complete Big6™ Skills #1–5 BEFORE you BEGIN your assignment. Complete Big6™ Skill #6 BEFORE you TURN IN your assignment.

Big6™ Skill #1: Task Definition

What does this assignment require me to do?

What information do I need in order to do this assignment?

Big6™ Skill #2: Information Seeking Strategies

What sources can I use to do the assignment?

Circle the best sources.

Big6™ Skill #3: Location & Access

Where can I find my sources?

Do I need help? If so, who can help me?

Big6™ Skill #4: Use of Information

What do I have to do with the information?

_____ read/view/listen _____ chart and/or write an essay

_____ take notes _____ copy and highlight

_____ answer questions _____ properly cite

_____ other: ______________________

Big6™ Skill #5: Synthesis

What product does this assignment require?

Big6™ Skill #6: Evaluation

Student self-evaluation checklist:

_____ I did what I was supposed to do (see Big6™ #1, Task Definition)

_____ The assignment is complete.

The Big6™ Eisenberg & Berkowitz, 1990. Assignment Organizer © Berkowitz & Hopsicker, 1997.

thought we were watering down the curriculum because we gave them the answers in the perfect chart. She didn't understand. It doesn't matter that we're giving them the content—it's the process that counts. We want them to actually spend more time concentrating on how to put [information] in their own words, and spend less time finding it. And, along the way, they are learning the content."

There were two kinds of evaluation: formative and summative. Formative involves diagnosing student performance during learning so that adjustments can be made before students turn in their work (or take a high-stakes exam!). Adjustments may include the following:

- Redirecting planned instruction to focus on areas in which students are having trouble
- Providing special learning activities not previously planned
- Helping students apply relevant technology tools
- Redefining the problem or returning to a previous Big6™ stage
- Offering one-on-one tutoring
- Brainstorming alternative approaches

Of course, the summative evaluation for this project was the Regents exam. It is vital to keep in mind the power of the affective side. All year long, we'd done this through confidence-building activities, daily quizzes, exposing students to high-quality work, and a number of other strategies. Perhaps the most amazing was the "Academic Pep Rally."

Picture the scene: 130 kids in the cafeteria, as Scott Hopsicker gives the Knute Rockne speech. "You've worked hard, and I believe in you. You will do well. If you get nervous, raise your hand. I won't be able to tell you the answer, but I'll stand beside you and give you my confidence."

Even now that Scott was lured away from Wayne Central and teaches in the Brockport (New York) Central School District, his results have followed him, as he puts the Big6™ process to the test, and his students continue to move ahead, pointing the way for the rest of us. You are the most crucial link for making these results happen in your school. We can improve scores by improving thinking!

Big6™ Skill 1: Task Definition

- To move from a 53% passing rate to the maximum possible
- To understand the tasks required of students by the Regents exam and prepare all students to succeed at every task
- To turn the exam into a learning experience

Big6™ Skill 2: Information-Seeking Strategies

To review and analyze all aspects of the teaching and learning process, Hopsicker and Berkowitz relied on multiple sources: review of lesson plans, curriculum, textbooks, classroom observations, and student journals. These were then compared to the performance tasks embedded in the Regents exam.

Big6™ Skill 3: Location and Access

How many kids truly engage with the information from the textbook? We created guided reading sections, with the 10–15 key sentences found in each section. Students would find key vocabulary, definitions, and explanations. They had to have those sheets with them to walk in the door. It was an easy way to get an A. Highlighting sections, underlining keywords on all multiple-choice worksheets, and tape-recording notes and then transcribing them—all contributed to strengthening these skills.

Big6™ Skill 4: Use of Information

Students must know what to do with information. Simply knowing the content is not enough. For example, students needed help with vocabulary contained within the questions, not just with the content. Knowing the difference between "identify and discuss" and "compare and contrast" involved learning the processes required for success. This skill had to be mastered first.

Big6™ Skill 5: Synthesis

Essay writing was the most difficult task for students. We provided tools, templates, and models to build their skills and confidence throughout the year.

Big6™ Skill 6: Evaluation

Evaluation was a continual process, leading up to the "main event" of the Regents exam itself. Students measured their own work against examples of quality work and learned to assess their efforts. More importantly, they came to understand their strengths and gaps and developed strategies that improved their performances.

Communications to the author may be addressed to Bob Berkowitz, Library Media Specialist, Wayne Central School, Route 350, Ontario Center, NY 14520; e-mail: Bberkowitz@wayne.k12.ny.us. For more information, visit <http://www.big6.com>.

Perfect Chart: Cases and Issues

McCulloch v. Maryland (1819)—federalism
Dred Scott v. Sanford (1857)—property rights
Plessy v. Ferguson (1896)—civil rights
Korematsu v. U.S. (1944)—Presidential power
Engel v. Vitale (1962)—freedom of religion
Miranda v. Arizona (1966)—due process

Choose all cases from the list. For each one chosen:

1. show how the constitutional issue listed was involved in the case,
2. state the Supreme Court's decision in the case, and
3. discuss an impact of the decision on United States history.

Case	How Constitutional Issue Was Involved	Supreme Court Decision	Impact of the Decision
McCulloch v. Maryland	Federalism = The division of power between state and national government Issue: Whether the state of Maryland could tax the National Bank.	Maryland could not tax the bank because it was created by the federal government.	Federal agencies are immune from control by the states.
Dred Scott v. Sanford	Issue: Whether Dred Scott could sue for his freedom because he was a slave.	Slaves are property, not citizens. Therefore slaves can't sue for their freedom.	Greater distrust between abolitionists and pro-slavery citizens, making compromises to avoid the Civil War worthless.
Plessy v. Ferguson	Issue: Whether separate facilities for blacks and whites were constitutional.	Separate, but equal is constitutional and it does not violate the 13th and 14th Amendments.	Separate facilities were not equal for blacks and the decision was later reversed by Brown v. Board of Education. Separate was not equal; segregation ended.
Korematsu v. U.S.	Issue: Whether the war powers of President FDR justified placing Japanese-Americans in internment camps.	Internment camps were justified because presidential powers expand during war or national crisis.	Rights of citizens can be suspended during war or national crisis.
Engel v. Vitale	Issue: Can schools force students to say a school prayer to start each day?	School prayer was contrary to the 1st Amendment because the Amendment provides for religious freedom but prevents government from establishing a religion.	A couple of Presidents since have called for a constitutional amendment allowing school prayer.
Miranda v. Arizona	Issue: Can the police deny you your right to an attorney during questioning?	The 5th Amendment protecting from self-incrimination and the 6th Amendment providing a right to an attorney were violated by the police when questioning Miranda.	All suspects must be read their rights when questioned and have the right to an attorney.

Part VIII: Curriculum Mapping

The Big6™ Curriculum Mapping

Introduction

In Part V, we noted that there are two levels of instructional design: micro and macro. In that section, we focused on the micro level in terms of lesson and unit design. Here, we go deeper into ways of implementing the Big6™ on the macro level. The intent is to facilitate integration of information skills instruction on the classroom, school, district, region, or even state level.

We continually stress that Big6™ instruction is fully compatible with existing subject area and classroom curriculum. The Big6™ provides students with the information understandings and skills necessary to carry out the various learning tasks provided by curriculum standards and frameworks. However, to successfully integrate Big6™ instruction requires accurate, up-to-date, and specific information about the curriculum on classroom, school, or district levels. In essence, we have an information problem of our own to solve—what is the "real" curriculum taught to students? We use the "Curriculum-Related Information Resources Brainstorming Sheet" provided in this section to brainstorm information seeking alternatives for curriculum information.

For example, school, district, or state curriculum guides are widely available sources of curriculum information. They provide some degree of detail on the curriculum as intended, but they do not provide specifics of the actual curriculum as experienced by students and teachers. Textbooks and Web sites may also provide usable curriculum information.

Curriculum Mapping

Since the mid-1970s, Mike has used a technique called "curriculum mapping" to gather, organize, and present reliable curriculum information. Curriculum mapping provides a mechanism for gathering specific and accurate information on the various attributes of classroom curriculum. The primary building block of curriculum in K–12 schools is the curriculum unit. Therefore, curriculum mapping is based on gathering data—generally from teachers but sometimes from students—about actual curriculum units or units intended for teaching.

Curriculum mapping involves two steps:

1. Systematically collecting information about what's actually going on in the classroom, and
2. Combining this information into charts and tables that describe the curriculum in a particular setting.

The "Curriculum Mapping Data Collection Worksheet" is the primary tool for gathering data on curriculum units. Multiple copies are provided so that audiences can experience the ease of filling out one or two and still have some left over. It only takes five to 10 minutes to complete a Curriculum Mapping Data Collection Worksheet. The Curriculum Mapping Data Collection Worksheet has undergone dozens of revisions over the years and should be individualized to local school settings. To save time and effort, no data should be gathered that is already available. School name, for example, should be already listed on the form, and the terms used to describe various teaching methods and assignments should reflect local vocabulary.

The Curriculum Mapping Data Collection Worksheet itself is not a curriculum map. A curriculum map is the compiled information from multiple worksheets. A blank form is provided to create a curriculum map, but this can also be accomplished using a computer database or electronic spreadsheet program. We also provide numerous examples of curriculum maps to show the usefulness and flexibility of the technique on the classroom, school, subject area, and district level as well as across grade levels—elementary, middle, and high school.

"Big Juicy" Units

Once maps are created, the task is to use the information in curriculum maps for planning Big6™ instruction that is integrated with classroom, subject area curriculum. Planning integrated instruction involves systematically reviewing the curriculum maps and selecting units that are best suited to integrated information and technology skills instruction. What we are trying to do is to identify the "big juicy" units, those information-rich curriculum units that are filled with information needs, resources, and processing. These are the units that offer particularly good opportunities for teaching specific Big6™ Skills within the overall Big6™ process.

For example, units that are good candidates for integrating Big6™ Skills instruction generally:

- Have a longer duration
- Involve a report, project, or product rather than a quiz or test
- Use multiple resources
- Involve a range of teaching methods

Big6™ Skills by Unit Matrix

Once desirable units are selected, they can be entered into the Big6™ Skills by Unit Matrix. If developed at the beginning of the school year, the Big6™ Skills by Unit Matrix becomes a blueprint for integrated information skills instruction. It can also be updated during the year to reflect what actually takes place. Finally, at the end of the year, the Matrix offers detailed documentation of what was actually accomplished. The Matrix also serves as the basis for follow-up planning by the teacher for the next year and for other teachers who will have the same students the next year.

Skills by Unit matrices can be created for individual teachers, teams, subject areas, schools, or even districts. Examples of various matrices are provided.

We cannot over-emphasize the importance of teaching all skills in context. The process of systematically reviewing curriculum, identifying valuable units for integrated instruction, and developing and documenting plans is important to a successful Big6™ program. The tools provided here give educators practical means for accomplishing meaningful, integrated Big6 classroom curriculum instruction.

Overview

Context

#1—The Process

- information problem solving—the Big6™

#2—Technology in Context

- technology in the process

#3—Curriculum

- real needs in real situations
- assignments: papers, reports, projects
- units and lessons

Context #1: The Process

1. Task Definition:
   1.1 Define the problem.
   1.2 Identify the information needed.
2. Information Seeking Strategies:
   2.1 Determine all possible sources.
   2.2 Select the best sources.
3. Location and Access:
   3.1 Locate sources.
   3.2 Find information within sources.
4. Use of Information:
   4.1 Engage (e.g., read, hear, view).
   4.2 Extract relevant information.
5. Synthesis:
   5.1 Organize information from multiple sources.
   5.2 Present information.
6. Evaluation:
   6.1 Judge the result (effectiveness).
   6.2 Judge the process (efficiency).

Context #2: Technology in a Big6™ Context

TASK DEFINITION	Students use e-mail, listservs, newsgroups, chat, videoconferencing, and other online communication methods to clarify assignments and brainstorm problems. May also use software to generate timelines, organizational charts, etc. to plan and organize complex problems.
INFO SEEKING	Students identify and assess computerized resources as they develop information seeking strategies toward their problem.
STRATEGIES LOCATION & ACCESS	Students use online catalogs, searchable periodical indexes, electronic encyclopedias, Web search engines, and other online searching tools to locate useful information.
USE OF INFORMA-TION	Students connect to and access online or locally stored electronic information sources, view, download, and decompress files, and use copy-and-paste features to extract relevant information.
SYNTHESIS	Students organize and communicate their results using word processing, database management, spreadsheet and graphics software, and distribute their projects via e-mail, Web publishing, or other media.
EVALUATION	Students evaluate the impact of the technology they used, including its effectiveness and efficiency. Students use e-mail, mailing lists, newsgroups, chat, videoconferencing, and other online communication methods to gain feedback from teachers.

Context #3: Curriculum

Real needs in real situations

- school, life, work
- assignments: papers, reports, projects
- integrated units and lessons

Curriculum—Big6™ Integration

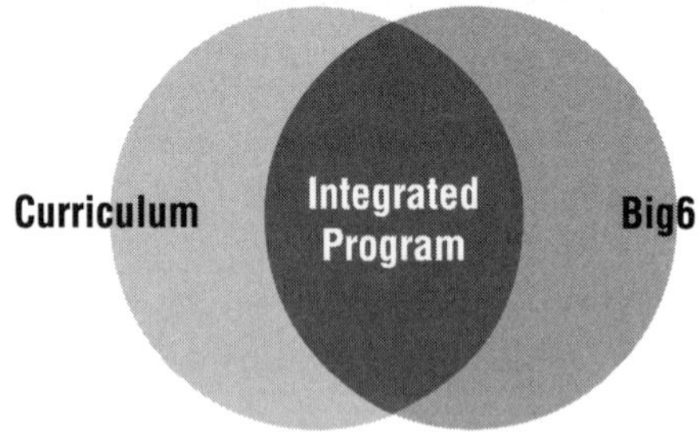

"Big Juicies" p. 144

Are important units in the curriculum:

- have a longer duration
- reach many students
- involve a report, project, or product
- use multiple resources
- involve a range of teaching methods

Curriculum Contexts

Math class working on graphs Social Studies discussion of current issues Science labs or projects English writing and vocabulary Health reports

Any assignment, particularly a project, report, or paper!!

Any personal decision that calls for information, e.g., selecting a TV show, buying a product...

The Big6™ Example: Assignment—Whales

GRADE 2	Create a picture book on whales
GRADE 5	Make a presentation (with multimedia aids) on types of whales and their habits.
GRADE 8	Projects: Are whales still endangered?
GRADE 12	Argumentative essay: Should Native Americans be allowed to hunt whales?

The Big6™ Examples (p. 174)

- 1st grade—language arts—ABC book
- 7th grade—Leon—recycling
- 10th grade—probability

The Big6™ Example: Freshman English Class

Information technology project

- Paper and oral presentations on the opportunities and challenges of living in the information age
- "Is freedom today and in the future enhanced or threatened by information and technology?"

The Big6™ Example (p. 174) 7th Grade Social Studies

- Leon
- Recycling project
- Short paper and oral presentation on the problems and solutions regarding recycling of one type of waste

Components of Integration

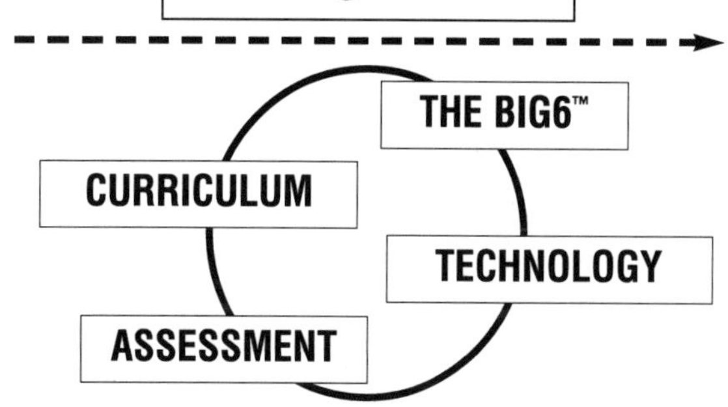

Curriculum Information—Information Seeking Strategies

Worksheet 8-1

Determine All Possible Sources	Select Best Sources

Integrating into the Curriculum: Curriculum Mapping

Data Collection Worksheet 8-2

School:		***Date:***	

Grade:		***Number of Sections:***	
Teacher:		***Number of Students:***	
Subject:		***Total Teaching Time:***	
Unit:		***Marking Period:***	

Level of Instruction:

- ❑ introduced
- ❑ reinforced
- ❑ expanded

Comment:

Resources:

- ❑ text
- ❑ one source
- ❑ multiple sources
  - ❑ reference (print/electr.)
  - ❑ periodicals
  - ❑ WWW
  - ❑ book (nonfiction)
  - ❑ book (fiction)
  - ❑ human
  - ❑ other:

Organization of Instruction:

- ❑ large group
- ❑ small group
- ❑ individual

Comment

Primary Teaching Method:

- ❑ desk work
- ❑ lecture
- ❑ demonstration
- ❑ video, film, multimedia
- ❑ lab, hands-on
- ❑ discussion
- ❑ independent study
- ❑ multimedia project
- ❑ report
- ❑ other:

Assignments:

- ❑ test
- ❑ short written assignment
- ❑ report
- ❑ project/product
- ❑ observation
- ❑ other:

Technologies:

- ❑ **tool** (word processing, database, presentation, spreadsheet)
- ❑ **communication** (e-mail, listserv, chat, video conferencing)
- ❑ **information** (web, database, electronlc resources, Q&A)
- ❑ other:

Relevant State/District Standards:

Comments:

Integrating into the Curriculum: Curriculum Mapping (cont.)

Data Collection Worksheet 8-2

School:	

Date:	

Grade:	
Teacher:	
Subject:	
Unit:	

Number of Sections:	
Number of Students:	
Total Teaching Time:	
Marking Period:	

Level of Instruction:
- ❑ introduced
- ❑ reinforced
- ❑ expanded

Comment:

Resources:
- ❑ text
- ❑ one source
- ❑ multiple sources
  - ❑ reference (print/electr.)
  - ❑ periodicals
  - ❑ WWW
  - ❑ book (nonfiction)
  - ❑ book (fiction)
  - ❑ human
  - ❑ other:

Organization of Instruction:
- ❑ large group
- ❑ small group
- ❑ individual

Comment

Primary Teaching Method:
- ❑ desk work
- ❑ lecture
- ❑ demonstration
- ❑ video, film, multimedia
- ❑ lab, hands-on
- ❑ discussion
- ❑ independent study
- ❑ multimedia project
- ❑ report
- ❑ other:

Assignments:
- ❑ test
- ❑ short written assignment
- ❑ report
- ❑ project/product
- ❑ observation
- ❑ other:

Technologies:
- ❑ **tool** (word processing, database, presentation, spreadsheet)
- ❑ **communication** (e-mail, listserv, chat, video conferencing)
- ❑ **information** (web, database, electronic resources, Q&A)
- ❑ other:

Relevant State/District Standards:

Comments:

Integrating into the Curriculum: Curriculum Mapping (cont.)

Data Collection Worksheet 8-2

School:	

Grade:	
Teacher:	
Subject:	
Unit:	

Level of Instruction:

- ❑ introduced
- ❑ reinforced
- ❑ expanded

Comment:

Resources:

- ❑ text
- ❑ one source
- ❑ multiple sources
  - ❑ reference (print/electr.)
  - ❑ periodicals
  - ❑ WWW
  - ❑ book (nonfiction)
  - ❑ book (fiction)
  - ❑ human
  - ❑ other:

Organization of Instruction:

- ❑ large group
- ❑ small group
- ❑ individual

Comment

Primary Teaching Method:

- ❑ desk work
- ❑ lecture
- ❑ demonstration
- ❑ video, film, multimedia
- ❑ lab, hands-on
- ❑ discussion
- ❑ independent study
- ❑ multimedia project
- ❑ report
- ❑ other:

Date:	

Number of Sections:	
Number of Students:	
Total Teaching Time:	
Marking Period:	

Assignments:

- ❑ test
- ❑ short written assignment
- ❑ report
- ❑ project/product
- ❑ observation
- ❑ other:

Technologies:

- ❑ **tool** (word processing, database, presentation, spreadsheet)
- ❑ **communication** (e-mail, listserv, chat, video conferencing)
- ❑ **information** (web, database, electronic resources, Q&A)
- ❑ other:

Relevant State/District Standards:

Comments:

Integrating into the Curriculum: Curriculum Mapping (cont.)

Data Collection Worksheet 8-2

School:	

Date:	

Grade:	
Teacher:	
Subject:	
Unit:	

Number of Sections:	
Number of Students:	
Total Teaching Time:	
Marking Period:	

Level of Instruction:
- ❑ introduced
- ❑ reinforced
- ❑ expanded

Comment:

Resources:
- ❑ text
- ❑ one source
- ❑ multiple sources
  - ❑ reference (print/electr.)
  - ❑ periodicals
  - ❑ WWW
  - ❑ book (nonfiction)
  - ❑ book (fiction)
  - ❑ human
  - ❑ other:

Organization of Instruction:
- ❑ large group
- ❑ small group
- ❑ individual

Comment

Primary Teaching Method:
- ❑ desk work
- ❑ lecture
- ❑ demonstration
- ❑ video, film, multimedia
- ❑ lab, hands-on
- ❑ discussion
- ❑ independent study
- ❑ multimedia project
- ❑ report
- ❑ other:

Assignments:
- ❑ test
- ❑ short written assignment
- ❑ report
- ❑ project/product
- ❑ observation
- ❑ other:

Technologies:
- ❑ **tool** (word processing, database, presentation, spreadsheet)
- ❑ **communication** (e-mail, listserv, chat, video conferencing)
- ❑ **information** (web, database, electronic resources, Q&A)
- ❑ other:

Relevant State/District Standards:

Comments:

Integrating into the Curriculum: Curriculum Mapping (cont.)

Data Collection Worksheet 8-2

School:	

Date:	

Grade:	
Teacher:	
Subject:	
Unit:	

Number of Sections:	
Number of Students:	
Total Teaching Time:	
Marking Period:	

Level of Instruction:
- ❑ introduced
- ❑ reinforced
- ❑ expanded

Comment:

Resources:
- ❑ text
- ❑ one source
- ❑ multiple sources
  - ❑ reference (print/electr.)
  - ❑ periodicals
  - ❑ WWW
  - ❑ book (nonfiction)
  - ❑ book (fiction)
  - ❑ human
  - ❑ other:

Organization of Instruction:
- ❑ large group
- ❑ small group
- ❑ individual

Comment

Primary Teaching Method:
- ❑ desk work
- ❑ lecture
- ❑ demonstration
- ❑ video, film, multimedia
- ❑ lab, hands-on
- ❑ discussion
- ❑ independent study
- ❑ multimedia project
- ❑ report
- ❑ other:

Assignments:
- ❑ test
- ❑ short written assignment
- ❑ report
- ❑ project/product
- ❑ observation
- ❑ other:

Technologies:
- ❑ **tool** (word processing, database, presentation, spreadsheet)
- ❑ **communication** (e-mail, listserv, chat, video conferencing)
- ❑ **information** (web, database, electronic resources, Q&A)
- ❑ other:

Relevant State/District Standards:

Comments:

Integrating into the Curriculum: Curriculum Mapping

Worksheet 8-3—Curriculum Map

GR TCHR	SUBJ	UNIT	#SEC	#STUD	TIME	MAR_PER	LEV	RES	ORG	METHODS	ASSIGN	TECH	Big6™	SERV	DATE

Worksheet 8-4—Sample Curriculum Map—All Fields Sorted by GR, SUBJ, MAR_P

GR	TCHR	SUBJ	UNIT	#SEC	#STUD	TIME	MAR_PER	LEV	RES	ORG	METHODS	ASSIGN	TECH	Big6™	SERV	DATE
00-00	LIE	LA	Colors	1	24	40	1234	I	mult	lg	disc/hands-on	worksheet	none			01/03/04
01-01	REB	LA	ABC book	1	25	15	x2xx	R/E	mult	lg/ind	demo/ind study	product	none			01/03/04
01-01	MAB	Math	Whole/Parts	1	32	10	x2xx	I	text/mult	lg	lect/desk work	worksheet	none			01/03/04
03-03	RDY	Sci	Planets	1	33	15	xx3x	I	mult	sg/lg	lect/group	project	WWW			01/03/04
03-03	RDY	Sci	Endangered Animals	1	33	15	xxx4	I	mult	lg/ind	lect/disc/ind	project	Hyperstudio/WWW			01/03/04
03-03	RDY	SS	Community	1	33	20	x2xx	R/E	mult	sg/lg	lect/disc/trip	project	Hyperstudio			01/03/04
03-04	CAL	LA	Letter Writing	1	27	8	x2xx	I	mult	ind	lect/desk work	product	w proc			09/27/03
03-04	CAL	Math	Graphs	1	27	15	xxx4	I	text	lg/ind	lect/desk work	product	none			09/27/03
03-04	CAL	Sci	Simple Machines	1	27	40	1xxx	I/R	text/mult	sg	lab/ind study	products	none			09/27/03
03-04	CAL	Sci	Work & Energy	1	27	8	xxx4	I	text	lg	lect	text	none			09/27/03
05-05	MBE	Library	Biography	5	120	2	xx3x	R/E	mult	lg	lect/disc	none	online catalog	1 2 3	res prov	01/03/04
06-06	SEW	LA	Folktales and Legends	1	29	20	x23x	R/E	mult	lg	lect/disc/ desk work	homework/test	none			01/03/04
06-06	SEW	Sci	Vocabulary	1	29	3	1xxx	R/E	text	lg/ind	lect/desk work	homework	none			01/03/04
06-06	SEW	SS	Current Events	1	29	40	1234	I/R/E	mult	lg/ind	disc/ind study	report	WWW			01/03/04
06-06	SEW	SS	Native Americans - Iroquois	1	29	10	x2xx	I	text	lg	lect/desk work	test	none			01/03/04

Worksheet 8-5a—Sample Curriculum Map—Includes a Product, Project, or Report

GR	TCHR	SUBJ	UNIT	#SEC	#STUD	TIME	MAR_PER	LEV	RES	ORG	METHODS	ASSIGN	TECH	Big6™	SERV	DATE
07-07	MBE	Library	Dictionary Skill	6	150	2	1xxx	R/E	one	lg	lect/desk work	swa	none	4		01/03/04
07-07	TMJ	Sci	Weather	3	87	15	xx3x	R/E	text	lg	lect/disc	test	none			01/03/04
07-07	TCH	SS	Recycling	3	87	15	x23x	R/E	mult	lg/ind	lect/ind	product	WWW/w proc/present/elec res, e-mail			01/03/04
08-08	TMJ	Sci	Noise	2	45	40	x2xx	R-E	mult	sg/lg/ind	demo/disc	written report	WWW/w pro/present/elec res			09/27/03
08-08	HJW	SS	Map Skills	4	111	10	1xxx	R/E	mult	lg	worksheet	worksheet	none			01/03/04
09-12	CER	Health	Diet & Nutrition	10	250	20	1x3x	R/E	mult	lg/sg	lect/disc/prod	posters	WWW/present			01/03/04
09-12	CER	Health	Tobacco & Smoking	10	250	10	1x3x	R/E	mult	lg/sg	lect/disc	test	none			01/03/04
09-12	CER	Health	Drugs	10	250	10	x2x4	R/E	mult	lg/sg	lect/disc/prod	product	WWW/present/ w proc			01/03/04
10-10	MBE	Library	Web authoring	9	20	10	x2xx	I	mult	ind	demo/prod/ind study	product (web page)	Front Page/ HTML/scanner	5		09/27/03
10-10	BAB	Math	Probability	4	104	20	xx3x	R/E	text	lg/ind	lect/desk work	homework	none			01/03/04
10-12	RBW	Physics	Light Lab	1	17	4	xx3x	I/R/E	laser, lab apparatus, text	lg - pairs	lect/lab	lab report	none			09/27/03
10-12	RBW	Physics	Light	1	17	15	xx3x	I/R/E	text	lg	lect/disc	test	none			09/27/03
11-12	CJC	LA	Catcher in the Rye	3	86	10	xx3x	I	mult	lg	lect/disc	report	none			09/27/03
11-12	MAB	Spanish 4	Spanish Cooking	1	14	10	xxx4	E	mult	ind	ind	product	WWW			01/03/04
11-12	BDE	SS	Supply & Demand	3	68	20	xx3x	I/R	mult	sg/lg	lect/disc	obs/swa	none			09/27/03

Worksheet 8-5b—Sample Curriculum Map—Includes of Product, Project, or Report

GR	TCHR	SUBJ	UNIT	#SEC	#STUD	TIME	MAR_PER	LEV	RES	ORG	METHODS	ASSIGN	TECH	Big6™	SERV	DATE
01-01	REB	LA	ABC book	1	25	15	x2xx	R/E	mult	lg/ind	demo/ind study	product	none			01/03/04
03-03	RDY	Sci	Planets	1	33	15	xx3x	I	mult	sg/lg	lect/group	project	WWW			01/03/04
03-03	RDY	Sci	Endangered Animals	1	33	15	xxx4	I	mult	lg/ind	lect/disc/ind	project	Hyperstudio/WWW			01/03/04
03-03	RDY	SS	Community	1	33	20	x2xx	R/E	mult	sg/lg	lect/disc/trip	project	Hyperstudio			01/03/04
03-04	CAL	LA	Letter Writing	1	27	8	x2xx	I	mult	ind	lect/desk work	product	w proc			09/27/03
03-04	CAL	Math	Graphs	1	27	15	xxx4	I	text	lg/ind	lect/desk work	product	none			09/27/03
03-04	CAL	Sci	Simple Machines	1	27	40	1xxx	I/R	text/mult	sg	lab/ind study	products	none			09/27/03
06-06	SEW	SS	Current Events	1	29	40	1234	I/R/E	mult	lg/ind	disc/ind study	report	WWW			01/03/04
07-07	TCH	SS	Recycling	3	87	15	x23x	R/E	mult	lg/ind	lect/ind	product	WWW/w proc/ present/elec res, e-mail			01/03/04
08-08	TMJ	Sci	Noise	2	45	40	x2xx	R-E	mult	sg/lg/ind	demo/disc	written report	WWW/w proc/ present/elec res, e-mail			09/27/03
09-12	CER	Health	Diet & Nutrition	10	250	20	1x3x	R/E	mult	lg/sg	lect/disc/prod	posters	WWW/present			01/03/04
09-12	CER	Health	Drugs	10	250	10	x2x4	R/E	mult	lg/sg	lect/disc/prod	product	WWW/present/ w proc			01/03/04
10-10	MBE	Library	Web authoring	9	20	10	x2xx	I	mult	ind	demo/prod/ind study	product (web page)	Front Page/ HTML/scanner	5		09/27/03
10-12	RBW	Physics	Light Lab	1	17	4	xx3x	I/R/E	laser, lab apparatus, text	lg - pairs	lect/lab	lab report	none			09/27/03
11-12	CJC	LA	Catcher in the Rye	3	86	10	xx3x	I	mult	lg	lect/disc	report	none			09/27/03
11-12	MAB	Spanish 4	Spanish Cooking	1	14	10	xxx4	E	mult	ind	ind	product	WWW			01/03/04

Worksheet 8-5c—Sample Secondary Map—Sorted by Number of Students and Time

#STUD	TIME	GR	TCHR	SUBJ	UNIT	#SEC	MAR_PER	LEV	RES	ORG	METHODS	ASSIGN	TECH	Big6™	SERV	DATE
250	20	09-12	CER	Health	Diet & Nutrition	10	1x3x	R/E	mult	lg/sg	lect/disc/prod	posters	WWW/present			01/03/04
250	10	09-12	CER	Health	Tobacco & Smoking	10	1x3x	R/E	mult	lg/sg	lect/disc	test	none			01/03/04
250	10	09-12	CER	Health	Drugs	10	x2x4	R/E	mult	lg/sg	lect/disc/prod	product	WWW/present/			01/03/04
150	2	07-07	MBE	Library	Dictionary Skill	6	1xxx	R/E	one	lg	lect/desk work	swa	none	4		01/03/04
111	10	08-08	HJW	SS	Map Skills	4	1xxx	R/E	mult	lg	worksheet	worksheet	none			01/03/04
104	20	10-10	BAB	Math	Probability	4	xx3x	R/E	text	lg/ind	lect/desk work	homework	none			01/03/04
87	15	07-07	TMJ	Sci	Weather	3	xx3x	R/E	text	lg	lect/disc	test	none			01/03/04
87	15	07-07	TCH	SS	Recycling	3	x23x	R/E	mult	lg/ind	lect/ind	product	WWW/w proc/ present/elec res, e-mail			01/03/04
86	10	11-12	CJC	LA	Catcher in the Rye	3	xx3x	I	mult	lg	lect/disc	report	none			09/27/03
68	20	11-12	BDE	SS	Supply & Demand	3	xx3x	I/R	mult	sg/lg	lect/disc	obs/swa	none			09/27/03
45	40	08-08	TMJ	Sci	Noise	2	x2xx	R-E	mult	sg/lg/ind	demo/disc	written report	WWW/w proc/ present/elec res			09/27/03
20	10	10-10	MBE	Library	Web authoring	9	x2xx	I	mult	ind	demo/prod/ind study	product (web page)	Front Page/ HTML/scanner	5		09/27/03
17	15	10-12	RBW	Physics	Light	1	xx3x	I/R/E	text	lg	lect/disc	test	none			09/27/03
17	4	10-12	RBW	Physics	Light Lab	1	xx3x	I/R/E	laser, lab apparatus, text	lg - pairs	lect/lab	lab report	none			09/27/03
14	10	11-12	MAB	Spanish 4	Spanish Cooking	1	xxx4	E	mult	ind	ind	product	WWW			01/03/04

Worksheet 8-5d—Sample Secondary Map—Sorted by Number of Students and Time

#STUD	TIME	GR	TCHR	SUBJ	UNIT	#SEC	MAR_PER	LEV	RES	ORG	METHODS	ASSIGN	TECH	Big6™	SERV	DATE
120	2	05-05	MBE	Library	Biography	5	xx3x	R/E	mult	lg	lect/disc	none	online catalog	1 2 3	res prov	01/03/04
33	20	03-03	RDY	SS	Community	1	x2xx	R/E	mult	sg/lg	lect/disc/trip	project	Hyperstudio			01/03/04
33	15	03-03	RDY	Sci	Planets	1	xx3x	I	mult	sg/lg	lect/group	project	WWW			01/03/04
33	15	03-03	RDY	Sci	Endangered Animals	1	xxx4	I	mult	lg/ind	lect/disc/ind	project	Hyperstudio/WWW			01/03/04
32	10	01-01	MAB	Math	Whole/Parts	1	x2xx	I	text/mult	lg	lect/desk work	worksheet	none			01/03/04
29	40	06-06	SEW	SS	Current Events	1	1234	I/R/E	mult	lg/ind	disc/ind study	report	WWW			01/03/04
29	20	06-06	SEW	LA	Folktales and Legends	1	x23x	R/E	mult	lg	lect/disc/desk work	homework/test	none			01/03/04
29	10	06-06	SEW	SS	Native Americans - Iroquois	1	x2xx	I	text	lg	lect/desk work	test	none			01/03/04
29	3	06-06	SEW	Sci	Vocabulary	1	1xxx	R/E	text	lg/ind	lect/desk work	homework	none			01/03/04
27	40	03-04	CAL	Sci	Simple Machines	1	1xxx	I/R	text/mult	sg	lab/ind study	products	none			09/27/03
27	15	03-04	CAL	Math	Graphs	1	xxx4	I	text	lg/ind	lect/desk work	product	none			09/27/03
27	8	03-04	CAL	LA	Letter Writing	1	x2xx	I	mult	ind	lect/desk work	product	w proc			09/27/03
27	8	03-04	CAL	Sci	Work & Energy	1	xxx4	I	text	lg	lect	text	none			09/27/03
25	15	01-01	REB	LA	ABC book	1	x2xx	R/E	mult	lg/ind	demo/ind study	product	none			01/03/04
24	40	00-00	LIE	LA	Colors	1	1234	I	mult	lg	disc/hands-on	worksheet	none			01/03/04

Worksheet 8-6
Sample Skills by Unit Matrix
Elementary School

The Big6™

GR	Tchr	Unit	Subject	Assignment	M_Per	1 Task Definition	2 Information Seeking Strategies	3 Location & Access	4 Use of Information	5 Synthesis	6 Evaluation	Comments
00-00	LIE	Colors	LA	worksheet	1234	X	x	x	X	X	X	Introduce the Super3 and overall process
01-01	REB	ABC book	LA	product	x2xx	X	x	x		X		Emphasize TD and Synthesis
01-01	MAB	Whole/Parts	Math	worksheet	x2xx				X		X	Use of worksheets
03-03	RDY	Community	SS	project	x2xx	X	X	x	x		x	Brainstorm and narrow—hit hard!
03-03	RDY	Planets	Sci	project	xx3x		X	X	x	X		Fun project, could use more time.
03-04	CAL	Simple Machines	Sci	products	1xxx	X				X		Different products
03-04	CAL	Graphs	Math	product	xxx4				X	X		Presentation in different formats
06-06	SEW	Current Events	SS	report	1234	X	X	X	X	X	X	All year long—can teach all Big6
06-06	SEW	Native Americans - Iroquois	SS	test	x2xx				X	X	X	Emphasizes the output side of the process

Worksheet 8-7
Sample Skills by Unit Matrix
Middle School

Sorted by grade level and marking period

The Big6™: 1 Task Definition; 2 Information Seeking Strategies; 3 Location & Access; 4 Use of Information; 5 Synthesis; 6 Evaluation

GR	Tchr	Unit	Subject	Assignment	QTR	1	2	3	4	5	6	Comments
06-06	SEW	Current Events	SS	report	1234	X	X	X	X	X	X	All year long - can hit all Big6
06-06	ARB	Poetry	English	short written assignment	xxx4				X	X	X	#4 - reading poems; #5/6 - writing good poetry
07-07	SLJ	Graphs	Math	product	x2xx				X	X		Types of graphs and spreadsheet software
07-07	TCH	Recycling	SS	product	x23x	X	X	X	-	X	-	Lots of technology
08-08	HJW	Map Skills	SS	worksheet	1xxx		X		X			Use of maps
08-08	TMJ	Noise	Sci	written report	x2xx	x	X	X		X	x	Build on gr 7, technology
07-08	CER	Diet and Nutrition	Health	posters	1x3x	X	X	-	-	X	x	Health reaches all students; repeats two times a year
07-08	CER	Tobacco and Smoking	Health	test	1x3x	X			X	X	X	"Cooperative teacher, test-taking." strategies & the Big6

Worksheet 8-8
Sample Skills by Unit Matrix
Secondary School

The Big6™

1 = Task Definition; 2 = Information Seeking Strategies; 3 = Location & Access; 4 = Use of Information; 5 = Synthesis; 6 = Evaluation

GR	Tchr	Unit	Subject	Assignment	M_Per	1	2	3	4	5	6	Comments
07-07	TCH	Recycling	SS	product	x23x	X	X	X	x	X	x	Lots of technology
08-08	HJW	Map Skills	SS	worksheet	1xxx		x		X			Use of maps
08-08	TMJ	Noise	Sci	written report	x2xx	x	X	X		X	x	Build on gr 7, technology
09-12	CER	Diet & Nutrition	Health	posters	1x3x	X	X	x	x	X	x	Health reaches all students; Repeats 2x year
09-12	CER	Tobacco & Smoking	Health	test	1x3x	X			X	X	X	Cooperative teacher, test-taking Strategies & the Big6
09-12	CER	Drugs	Health	product	x2x4	X	x	x	x	x	X	
11-12	CJC	Catcher in the Rye	LA	report	xx3x		X	X				Literacy criticism resources
11-12	BDE	Supply & Demand	SS	obs/swa	xx3x	X	X	X				First effort with this teacher

Worksheet 8-9
Sample Skills by Unit Matrix
Mr. Hancock—4th Grade Teacher

The Big6™: 1 Task Definition, 2 Information Seeking Strategies, 3 Location & Access, 4 Use of Information, 5 Synthesis, 6 Evaluation

Unit	Subject	Assignment	M_Per	Pers	1	2	3	4	5	6	Comments
Spelling	Language Arts	Test	1234	40				X	x		Strategies for learning/remembering spelling
State History	Social Studies	Written Report	12xx	30	X	X	X	X	X	X	Major unit - lessons on all Big6
Geography	Social Studies	Maps, Product	1x3x	20	X				X		Computer graphics to produce maps
Listening Skills	Language Arts	Test	1xxx	10	X			X			Note-taking, tape recording
Personal Hygiene	Health	Ads, Product	1xxx	15	X	x			x	X	Evaluating ads, creating posters
Letter Writing	Language Arts	Product	1xxx	15	X				X	X	What makes a good letter? Using word processing.
Food Groups	Health	Product (chart, posters, ads)	x2xx	15	X	X	X	X			Periodical indexes on CD and the Web
Multiplication Tables-10s	Math	Test	x2xx	20				x			Just mention ways to memorize
Structure of Plants	Science	"Experiment, Test"	xx34	20					X		Lab reports - can computer generate
Rocks and Minerals	Science	"Worksheet, Test"	xx3x	20		X	X				Use sources for worksheet—focus on brainstorm, narrow, and keywords
Metric Measurements	Math	Test	xx3x	20		X	X				Test will include examples of the metric system in action. Will need sources.
Deserts/Life, Weather	Social Studies/ Science	Written and Oral Report	xx3x	30	X	X	X				Two subjects, lots of electronic information seeking strategies, location & access
Mixed Numbers	Math	Worksheet	xx3x	20						X	Self-evaluation

Worksheet 8-10
Sample Skills by Unit Matrix
Social Studies Department

The Big6™

GR	Tchr	Unit	Subject	Assignment	M_Per	1 Task Definition	2 Information Seeking Strategies	3 Location & Access	4 Use of Information	5 Synthesis	6 Evaluation	Comments
9	Sullivan	Latin America	Social Studies	Test	1xxx	X	x	x	x	X	X	Test taking strategies—Task Definition, Synthesis
9	Sullivan	Northern Africa	Social Studies	"Test, Report"	x2xx		X	X	X		x	Sources - web searching, note-taking
9	Sullivan	India	Social Studies	"Maps, Product"	xx3x					X		Computer software to create various kinds of maps
10	Ryan	WW I	Social Studies	Test	1xxx	X				X		
10	Ryan	Between the Wars	Social Studies	Test, Short Written Assignment	12xx					X		Essay writing strategies
10	Ryan	WW II	Social Studies	"Project, Test"	x2xx		X	X	x	x		Web-based information
10	Ryan	Cold War	Social Studies	Test	xx3x						X	
10	Ryan	Vietnam	Social Studies	Oral Report	xx34		x	x	X	X	x	Presentation and graphics software
11	Rossini	Colonization of Western Hem.	Social Studies	Test	1xxx	X			X			Extracting relevant information from the textbook and notes
11	Rossini	Civil War	Social Studies	"Report, Project"	xx3x		X	X	X			Using primary and secondary sources
11	Jackson	Constitution	Social Studies	Written and Oral Report	x2xx					X	X	Presentation software (PowerPoint)
11	Jackson	Civil War	Social Studies	Test	xx3x	X						Nature of test
12	Petruso	Street Law	Social Studies	Project	xxx4		X			X		Community resources and law libraries
12	Valesky	Stock Market	Social Studies	Project	1234	X	X	X	x	x	X	Full-year, competitive intelligence

Worksheet 8-11
Skills by Unit Matrix

The Big6™

1 Task Definition
2 Information Seeking Strategies
3 Location & Access
4 Use of Information
5 Synthesis
6 Evaluation

GR	Tchr	Unit	Subject	Assignment	M_Per	1	2	3	4	5	6	Comments

Worksheet 8-12
Services by Unit Matrix

						Information, Library, and Technology Services						
						Resources Provision	Facilities Provision	Reading/Media Guidance	Information Services	Skills Instruction	Info/Curriculum Consultation	
GR	**Tchr**	**Unit**	**Subject**	**Assignment**	**M_Per**	**RP**	**FP**	**RG**	**IS**	**SI**	**ICC**	**Comments**

Worksheet 8-13—Big6™ Curriculum—Year Timeline Planner (K-12)

GR	Tchr	Subject	Assignment	Weeks 1–39	The Big6™ 1	2	3	4	5	6
00-00	LIE	LA	worksheet	**COLORS**	X	x	x	X	X	X
01-01	REB	LA	product		X	x	x		X	
01-01	MAB	Math	worksheet	ABC Book				X		X
03-03	RDY	SS	project	COMMUNITY****	X	X	x	x		x
03-03	RDY	Sci	project	**PLANETS**		X	X	x	X	
03-04	CAL	Sci	products	SIMPLE MACHINES*****	X				X	
03-04	CAL	Math	product	GRAPHS				X	X	
06-06	SEW	SS	report	***Current Events**	X	X	X	X	X	X
06-06	SEW	SS	test	IROQUOIS****				X	X	X
07-07	TCH	SS	product	RECYCLING	X	X	X	x	X	x
08-08	HJW	SS	worksheet	Map Skills		x		X		
08-08	TMJ	Sci	wr report	NOISE*********************	x	X	X		X	x
09-12	CER	Health	posters	Diet/Nutrition … Diet/Nutrition	X	X	x	x	X	x
09-12	CER	Health	test	Smoking … Smoking	X			X	X	X
09-12	CER	Health	product	DRUGS** … DRUGS**	X	x	x	x	x	X
11-12	CJC	LA	report	Catcher/Rye		X	X			
11-12	BDE	SS	obs/swa	Supply & Demand**	X	X	X			

Worksheet 8-14—Big6™ Curriculum—Year Timeline Planner (K-12)

																																												The Big6™					
GR	Tchr	Subject	Assignment	1		3		5		7		9		11		13		15		17		19		21		23		25		27		29		31		33		35		37		39		1	2	3	4	5	6

Part IX: The Parent Connection

The Parent Connection

Introduction

This part of the Workshop Handbook focuses on the parent or caregiver connection. Parents and caregivers can be important partners for educators in helping students to gain information skills and to succeed in school. We often hold parent/community workshops and sessions to encourage parents to get involved and to do so in constructive and meaningful ways. We find that parents are eager audiences and we encourage using the materials in this section (as well as our *Helping With Homework* book) to conduct your own parent/community sessions.

Big6™ Parent Workshop: How to Get Started

These sessions do not need to be long—one hour maximum or even as short as 15–20 minutes. The point is to help parents understand the Big6™ themselves and then learn to guide their children through assignments and tasks using the Big6™. Our sessions usually take the following outline:

- The information age: Implications for learning & teaching
- Information literacy: The Big6™ Skills process & approach
- The parent role
- The technology connection
- Q&A

Materials and Exercises

The materials in this part of the Workshop Handbook are also designed for use in parent/community sessions.

The "Overview" slides are used to explain the parent role. We emphasize that parents can help and use the Big6™ at three different points in time:

- Before their children actually start their homework—by talking the students through the process
- During the work — by troubleshooting with their children if they get stuck
- After their children are finished — by checking their work

The detailed chart, "Helping With Homework," provides three different examples of guiding and coaching. We find it really helps adult audiences to understand how to use the Big6™ to guide students.

Two exercises are provided to further develop guiding and coaching skills. One exercise deals with a single assignment (the astronomy paper) while the other offers scenarios from a variety of situations. We sometimes break parent/community audiences into groups, work through the exercises, and then discuss with the full audience.

The "Hopsicker Letter" is an example of communication from a teacher to parents explaining the information skills — classroom connection. The "Helping With Homework: A Big6™ Assignment Organizer" is a useful tool for helping students to stay on top of their assignments.

Lastly, the ERIC Digest, "Helping With Homework: A Parent's Guide to Information Problem-Solving," brings it all together. The digest may be copied and distributed at presentations.

Parents Can Guide and Coach

Parents and caregivers can and should play an important role in helping their children succeed. However, while well-intentioned in providing assistance, parents often lack the necessary understandings and approaches to truly help. In fact, many times, parent-children help sessions wind up in conflict and confrontation.

We encourage parents to avoid confrontation by using the Big6™ to help guide or coach. With the Big6™, parents are not being asked to teach, as that usually leads to their children exclaiming "that's not the way my teacher does it!" Rather, the parents are guiding their children on teacher-determined, established goals and curriculum.

Overview

Information and Technology Skills for Student Success: The Big6™ Skills Approach

The Parent Connection: Helping with Homework

"Parents can make a difference by helping, not by teaching or doing."

—from *Helping with Homework*, 1997

Parents can assist children to learn how to approach information problems (both in and out of school) and to choose the tools to solve those problems.

Approach for Parents

Parent as helper-guide

- before homework: talk through
- during homework: troubleshoot
- after homework: check

Using the Big6™ Process

- a tool for solving information problems
- context for use of technology

Information Problem-Solving in School, Life, and Work Contexts

Information Problem-Solving Process	1st Grade Language Arts—Maria's homework is to make an ABC book.	7th Grade Social Studies—Leon has to do a social studies report (three minute oral with visual aids) on recycling.	10th Grade Math—Joanne is working on probability homework problems. She missed two days of school this week.
Task Definition	■ After the teacher explains the assignment, Maria decides that she will make an ABC book based on the topic of food. In talking with her mother, she realizes she will need to gather lots of foods (and spellings).	■ Leon decides to narrow the topic of recycling to investigate ways of recycling tires.	■ Joanne realizes that because she missed school, she doesn't really know how to do the problems assigned.
Information Seeking Strategies	■ Maria decides to ask her mother for help in getting information about foods. Together they realize that a cookbook might help and that maybe she can find one for kids in the library media center.	■ Leon talks to the school library media specialist about his idea. She suggests using CD-ROM magazine indexes and searching the World Wide Web as two good sources.	■ Joanne asks her older brother what she should do. He asks what the teacher relies on most—the textbook or class notes. Joanne says that the class notes are most important.
Location & Access	■ The library media specialist helps Maria to find a children's cookbook.	■ Leon searches using the Magazine Articles Summaries CD-ROM and also searches the World Wide Web using Yahoo.	■ Joanne calls her friend Tonya and arranges to go over to her house to look over her notes.
Use of Information	■ Maria reads through the book to find the names of fruits, vegetables, and other foods. She writes each name on a card.	■ Leon reads the articles on the screen and is able to cut and paste directly into his word processor.	■ Tonya explains how the notes are organized and shows Joanne the pages that specifically relate to the homework. Joanne copies Tonya's notes.
Synthesis	■ Maria uses pictures from magazines, construction paper, and crayons to illustrate her book. She puts all the pages in alphabetical order and staples them together. Maria practices reading her ABC book to her mother.	■ He practices his presentation. He makes a few changes in order to be more specific about the benefits of recycling tires.	■ Joanne is able to do three of the problems but gets stuck on the other three. She writes a note on her homework that she needs additional help.
Evaluation	■ Maria decides that she likes her book but that coming up with an idea for the letter "X" was hard.	■ Leon reviews his draft and realizes he has plenty of specific information on recycling tires but needs to add more general information about recycling in the introduction.	■ Joanne realizes that she still needs direct information from her teacher and arranges to come in for extra help.

Worksheet 9-1a—Parent Exercises

Big6™ Skills: Developing an Understanding in Context

Parent Exercise: The Astronomy Paper. Your child is studying astronomy. The assignment is to write a paper about a trip to a planet or other body in the solar system. Please try to identify the relevant Big6™ stage and note possible actions that you might take. Note: There are six situations, one for each Big6™.

Situation	Big6™	Your Possible Actions
Your child says, "I can't find anything about Mars. How am I supposed to do this project anyway?"		
Your child is confused about exactly what to do and asks, "Isn't this just a typical astronomy report?" What do you do?		
Your child is having trouble creating a picture using a paint program. What can you do?		
Your child is having trouble reading from your neighbor's college astronomy textbook. How can you help?		
Your child asks you to check to see if all the necessary parts are included. What do you do?		
Your child is having trouble finding information on Callisto in the encyclopedia. How can you help?		

Big6™ Skills

1. **Task Definition**
   1.1 Define the problem.
   1.2 Identify the information needed.
2. **Information Seeking Strategies**
   2.1 Determine all possible sources.
   2.2 Select the best source.
3. **Location & Access**
   3.1 Locate sources.
   3.2 Find information within sources.
4. **Use of Information**
   4.1 Engage (e.g., read, hear, view).
   4.2 Extract relevant information.
5. **Synthesis**
   5.1 Organize information from multiple sources.
   5.2 Present the result.
6. **Evaluation**
   6.1 Judge the result (effectiveness).
   6.2 Judge the process (efficiency).

Worksheet 9-1b—Big6™ Skills: Developing an Understanding in Context

General Exercise: Parent-Student Interactions. Below are examples of problems students might have in a variety of situations. Please try to identify the relevant Big6™ Skill and note possible actions that you might take. Note: More than one Big6™ may apply to a given situation and not all Big6™ are necessarily used.

Situation	Big6™	Your Possible Actions
Your 11th grade daughter is flipping through a thick guide to colleges. She's frustrated and anxious and says, "Maybe I just won't go to college."		
Your son is working on a 4th grade science experiment. He asks for help because he doesn't know how he should take notes on his observations.		
Your daughter and her friend complain that they don't know what's on tomorrow's test.		
Your son just finished his literary criticism paper. You ask, "How did you do?" He responds, "I haven't got a clue."		
You rush in the room after your daughter screams, "I just can't do this!" You see her staring at the shoebox full of note cards for her geography report.		
Calvin says, "If I had a computer, I'm sure I'd get better grades on my book reports."		

Big6™ Skills

1. **Task Definition**
   1.1 Define the problem.
   1.2 Identify the information needed.
2. **Information Seeking Strategies**
   2.1 Determine all possible sources.
   2.2 Select the best source.
3. **Location & Access**
   3.1 Locate sources.
   3.2 Find information within sources.
4. **Use of Information**
   4.1 Engage (e.g., read, hear, view).
   4.2 Extract relevant information.
5. **Synthesis**
   5.1 Organize information from multiple sources.
   5.2 Present the result.
6. **Evaluation**
   6.1 Judge the result (effectiveness).
   6.2 Judge the process (efficiency).

Hopsicker Letter

SAMPLE • SAMPLE • SAMPLE • SAMPLE • SAMPLE • SAMPLE • SAMPLE

Mr. Scott Hopsicker
Wayne Central High School
Social Studies Department

October 8, 2003

Dear Parent or Guardian,

As a teacher, and more importantly your student's Social Studies teacher, I know that parents/guardians can be key partners in helping their children be successful in school. I am asking for your help because parents/guardians can provide an atmosphere which fosters achievement and success. However, the question is, "What can parents/guardians do to help their students that will have the biggest impact?" Answer: Assignments — especially homework.

U.S. History and Government is designed to be a conceptual course aimed at giving students an understanding of events and issues that impact social, political, economic, and foreign policy concerns. The course covers such topics as: the constitution, impact of the presidents, and supreme court cases throughout America's history. Homework is assigned on a regular basis. Assignments are ways for my students to show me what they know. They are also ways for students to learn, review, remediate, or extend what is taught in my classroom. To be successful on quizzes and tests in this course, the homework must be done.

You can help your students be successful with their homework assignments by guiding, assisting, and generally making it easier for them to succeed. The attached "Homework Planner" offers a framework that you can use to guide students through assignments and homework. I think that this simple tool can make a big difference. I will make copies available for all students and encourage that they be used to help organize homework assignments. I hope you will help me by using this organizer with your student whenever he or she has homework in U.S. History and Government.

Please feel free to contact me at the high school whenever you have any concerns. If you leave a message at the main office, I will return your call as soon as possible.

Thank you in advance for your support and cooperation.

Sincerely,

Scott Hopsicker

Reprinted with author's permission.

SAMPLE • SAMPLE • SAMPLE • SAMPLE • SAMPLE • SAMPLE • SAMPLE

Worksheet 9-2—Helping With Homework: A Big6™ Assignment Organizer

Assignment: ______________________________ **Date Due:** ________________

Complete Big6™ Skills #1-5 BEFORE you BEGIN your assignment.
Complete Big6™ Skill #6 BEFORE you TURN IN your assignment.

Big6™ Skill #1: Task Definition

What does this assignment require me to do?

What information do I need in order to do this assignment?

Big6™ Skill #2: Information Seeking Strategies	**Big6™ Skill #3: Location & Access**
What sources can I use to do the assignment? Circle the best sources.	Where can I find my sources? Do I need help? If so, who can help me?

Big6™ Skill #4: Use of Information

What do I have to do with the information?

______ read/view/listen
______ take notes
______ answer questions
______ other: ____________________
______ chart and/or write an essay
______ copy and highlight
______ properly cite

Big6™ Skill #5: Synthesis

What product does this assignment require?

Big6™ Skill #6: Evaluation

Student self-evaluation checklist:

_____ I did what I was supposed to do (see Big6™ #1, Task Definition)
_____ The assignment is complete.

ERIC

ERIC Digest

ERIC Clearinghouse on Information
& Technology at Syracuse University
621 Skytop Road, Suite 160
Syracuse, New York 13244
www.ericit.org
EDO-IR-2002-04

November 1996 EDO-IR-96-09

Helping With Homework: A Parent's Guide to Information Problem-Solving

By Robert E. Berkowitz

This Digest is based on the book, Helping With Homework: A Parent's Guide to Information Problem-Solving, *by Michael B. Eisenberg & Robert E. Berkowitz*

Introduction

Parents can play an important role in helping their children succeed in school, but they need an effective approach in order to do this well. The approach taken in the book, *Helping with Homework: A Parent's Guide to Information Problem-Solving*, is based on the Big6™ Skills problem-solving approach. The Big6™ Skills apply to any problem or activity that requires a solution or result based on information. An abundance of information is available from many sources, and the Big6™ can help parents effectively deal with that information to guide their youngsters through school assignments.

The Big6™ Approach

The Big6™ approach has six components: task definition, information seeking strategies, location and access, use of information, synthesis, and evaluation.

- Task Definition: In the task definition stage, students need to determine what is expected from the assignment.
- Information Seeking Strategies: Once students know what's expected of them, they need to identify the resources they will need to solve the task as defined. This is information seeking.
- Location & Access: Next, the students must find potentially useful resources. This is location and access — the implementation of the information seeking strategy.
- Use of Information: Use of information requires the students to engage the information (e.g., read it) and decide how to use it (e.g., in text or in a footnote).
- Synthesis: Synthesis requires the students to repackage the information to meet the requirements of the task as defined.
- Evaluation: Finally, students need to evaluate their work on two levels before it is turned in to the teacher. Students need to know if their work will meet their teacher's expectations for (1) quality and (2) efficiency.

The Big6™ steps may be applied in any order, but all steps must be completed.

Parents' Role and Students' Role

The Big6™ approach requires parents and students to assume different roles. The parent assumes the role of a "coach" and the child assumes the role of "thinker and doer." As a coach, the parent can use the Big6™ Skills to guide the student through all the steps it takes to complete the assignment. Parents can help by first asking their children to explain assignments in their own words. This is "task definition"—a logical first step. Parents can also help by discussing possible sources of information. This is "information seeking strategies." Parents can then help their children implement information seeking strategies by helping their children find useful resources. This is the Big6™ step called "location and access." Location and access may have to be repeated during an assignment because some children may not identify everything they need right at the beginning. Parents can facilitate by brainstorming with their children alternate places where information might be available. In the "use of information" stage, parents can discuss whether the information the child located is relevant and if so, help the child decide how to use it. In the "synthesis" stage, parents can ask for a summary of the information in the child's own words and ask whether the information meets the requirements identified in the "task definition" stage. The end of any assignment is the final check, an evaluation of all the work that has been done. Parents can help their children with the "evaluation" stage by discussing whether the product answers the original question, whether it meets the teacher's expectations, and whether the project could have been done more efficiently.

As children work through each of the Big6™ steps, they need to think about what they need to do, and then they need to find appropriate ways to do it. This is their role — "thinker and doer." Children should be encouraged to be as independent as possible, but they will often have difficulty beginning an assignment because they are confused about what is expected of them. Whatever the reason is for their inability to get started, students have the ultimate responsibility for getting their work done. When parents act as coaches, they can help their children assume this responsibility by engaging them in conversation about what is expected of them, and then by guiding them throughout the assignment using the Big6™ Skills.

Why Assignments?

Assignments provide students with an opportunity to review and practice new material, to correct errors in understanding and production, and to assess levels of mastery. Every assignment is an information problem that can be solved using the Big6™. For instance, the goal of many assignments is to have the students practice a skill taught in class. If a child is having a problem understanding an assignment, the parent may help by encouraging the child to explain what it is he or she does not understand. The parent can use information seeking strategies to help the child identify information sources by asking questions such as: "Is there another student in your class who can help you understand how to do this?" or, "Did the teacher give any other examples?" The parent can help the child identify information sources and suggest ways to get them. For instance, the public television network may have a homework hotline, the public library may have study guides, or a neighborhood child may be in the same class.

Technology and The Big6™

The Big6™ approach recognizes the benefits of technology in education because computers are tools that help organize information. Software programs do a variety of functions such as edit written work, check grammar and spelling, chart and graph quantities, and construct outlines. Computers can also help with time management, setting priorities, and evaluating efficiency.

Using the Internet, students can connect to many non-traditional sources of information and are not limited to information contained on library shelves. They can use e-mail to talk directly with specialists and experts who can add a personal dimension to an assignment.

Conclusion

It is an axiom of American education that parents are partners in their children's education. Parents have traditionally participated by helping their children with homework. The Big6™ approach can help parents effectively guide their children through assignments and at the same time help their children become independent learners and users of information.

Bibliography

Eisenberg, M. B. & Berkowitz, R. E. (1990). *Information problem solving: The Big6™ Skills approach to library and information skills instruction.* Norwood, NJ: Ablex. Ablex Publishing Corporation, 355 Chestnut St. Norwood, NJ 07648 ($22.95). Document not available from EDRS. (ED 330 364)

Eisenberg, M. B. & Berkowitz, R. E. (1992). Information problem-solving: The Big6™ Skills approach. *School Library Media Activities Monthly, 8* (5), 27–29,37,42. (EJ 438 023)

Eisenberg, M. B. & Berkowitz, R. E. (1995, August). The six study habits of highly effective students: Using the Big6™ to link parents, students, and homework. *School Library Journal, 41* (8), 22-25. (EJ 510 346)

Eisenberg, M. B. & Spitzer, K. L. (1991, Oct.) Skills and strategies for helping students become more effective information users. *Catholic Library World, 63* (2), 115–120. (EJ 465 828)

Granowsky, A. (1991). What parents can do to help children succeed in school. *PTA Today, 17* (1), 5–6. (EJ 436 757)

Indiana State Department of Education. (1990). *Get ready, get set, parent's role: Parent booklet.* [Booklet]. Indianapolis, IN: Author. (ED 337 264)

Konecki, L. R. (1992). *Parent talk: Helping families relate to schools and facilitate children's learning.* Paper presented at the Annual Meeting of the Association of Teacher Educators (Orlando, FL, February 17, 1992). (ED 342 745)

Lankes, R. D. (1996). *The bread & butter of the Internet: A primer and presentation packet for educators.* (IR-101). Syracuse, NY: ERIC Clearinghouse on Information & Technology. (ED 402 924)

Scarnati, J. T. & Platt, R. B. (1991, Oct.) Lines and pies and bars, oh my! Making math fun. *PTA Today, 17* (1), 9–11. (EJ 436 759)

Van, J. A. (1991, Oct.). Parents are part of the team at Hearst Award Winner's school. *PTA Today, 17* (1), 7–8. (EJ 436 758)

This ERIC Digest was prepared by Robert E. Berkowitz, K–12 coordinator of library programs at Wayne Central School District in Ontario Center, NY, and adjunct instructor at Syracuse University's School of Information Studies.

ERIC Clearinghouse on Information & Technology, 621 Skytop Road, Suite 160, Syracuse University, Syracuse, NY 13244-4100; (315) 443-3640; Fax: (315) 443-5448; e-mail: eric@ericir.syr.edu; or URL: <http://ericit.org>.

This publication was prepared with funding from the Office of Educational Research and Improvement, U.S. Department of Education, under contract no. RR93002009. The opinions expressed in this report do not necessarily reflect the positions of OERI or ED.

Library Media Connection

LMC
LIBRARY MEDIA CONNECTION

The Professional Magazine for School Library Media Specialists

Library Media Connection is written by library media professionals for library professionals. Our writers and editors are the leaders in library science, the speakers you love to hear at conferences, and your valued colleagues. They include Kathy Schrock, Doug Johnson, Gary Hartzell, Michael Eisenberg, and Carol Simpon, among others.

I year subscription just $69.00

ORDER FORM

Date_______________ Purchase Order#_______________ Source_______________

BILL TO:

____
Attention ***(verify spelling)***

____
Title

____
District/School Name

____
Address

____
City State Zip + 4

☐ MasterCard ☐ VISA Expiration Date_____/_____

__ __ __ __ __ __ __ __ __ __ __ __ __ __ __ __
Charge Card Account#

____
Signature

SHIP TO:

____
Name ***(verify spelling)***

____
Title

____
District/School Name

____
Address

____
City State Zip + 4

Person Placing Order______________________________

Phone #______________________________

QTY	BIG6 TITLES	PRICE	AMOUNT
	B6B Big6 Bookmarks (250 pk)	29.95	
	978 Big6 Collection	39.95	
	811 Big6 in Elementary Schools	39.95	
	066 Big6 in Secondary Schools	39.95	
	B6P Big6 Poster—Elementary	15.95	
	B62 Big6 Poster—Secondary	15.95	
	BSB Big6 Poster Cards (100 pk)	12.95	
	B6V Big6 Video: Essential Skills	85.00	
	86X Curriculum Initiative	58.50	
	422 Helping With Homework	34.95	
	575 Information Problem Solving	38.95	
	940 Internet Power Research	17.95	
	Solving Information Problems Video	95.00	
	074 Using the Big6 to Teach	39.95	

Subtotal (Subscriptions) .... $ ______
Subtotal (Books) .... $ ______
Shipping & Handling (Books)..................... $ ______
TAX (Ohio orders only) Tax Exempt#______________ $ ______
TOTAL AMOUNT DUE $

Linworth
PUBLISHING, INC

To order: Linworth Publishing, Inc
480 E Wilson Bridge Rd., Suite L
Worthington, OH 43085
Call: 800-786-5017,
Fax: 614-436-9490,
or order on line: www.linworth.co

Your Library-to-Classroom Connection with Books, Magazines, and Online

Part X: Big6™ Program Planning

Big6™ Program Planning

Introduction

After working through the worksheets, exercises, and readings in this Handbook, you should be well-informed about the Big6™ process and approach. You should also have some conceptual frameworks and practical methods for planning and implementing Big6™ Skills instruction on the district, school, and classroom levels.

The Big6™ is an approach to information and technology skills instruction that puts students in a position to be successful information problem-solvers. In the Handbook, we emphasized:

- The nature and scope of the Big6™ Skills
- The purpose and use of curriculum maps for planning integrated curriculum
- Needs and mechanisms for instructional design and planning on the macro and micro levels
- The role of assessment in terms of efficiency and effectiveness
- Collaborative roles for all educators as well as parents, community members, and even students in implementing meaningful Big6™ instruction

Long-Term Planning

What remains is to look ahead and more formally plan for the future; to take all of these parts and forge them into a cohesive whole. This requires:

- Assessing the current status of your own level of expertise as well as the status of integrated skills instruction at the school or district level

- Determining what is desirable in terms of meeting students' needs to attain Big6™ Skills
- Determining what it will take in terms of curriculum, technology, and planning to meet students needs
- Establishing a timeframe for accomplishing these goals

In Part X, we provide forms and charts to begin this kind of long-term planning for effective Big6™ Skills instruction. These tools will help you to analyze students' needs as well as the status of personal, school, and district inputs. They provide a mechanism to gauge the extent of your own expertise, the needs of students, and the current degree of the school community's cooperation. You can then use this base to plan for further personal and systemic development.

We urge you to "think big!" Information and technology skills instruction is not optional; it's not an add-on. Big6™ Skills instruction is part of a basic skills education in the 21st century.

To borrow from the mission statement of the American Association of School Librarians and the Association for Educational Communications and Technology, our goal is "to ensure that students are effective users of ideas and information" (*Information Power*, 1988, p. 1; 1998, p. 6).

We are confident that you will use the ideas, strategies, and tools offered in this handbook to make a difference in your schools and communities. We encourage you to customize and personalize the various forms and activities in order to envision, analyze, plan, implement, and evaluate on your own.

Again—think Big(6)!

Worksheet 10-1—Personal Planning

	Current Status	Needs	Time Frame
Curriculum: Instructional Design			
Big6™ Information and Technology Skills			
Technology: Personal Skills			
Technology: Context			
Planning: Micro			
Planning: Macro			

Worksheet 10-2—School or District Planning

	Current Status	Needs	Time Frame
Student Skills and Needs			
Curriculum			
Big6™ Information and Technology Skills Instruction			
Technology			
Planning: Macro			

Worksheet 10-3—Assessment: Big6™—Big View

1. Determine key indicators for a quality Big6™ program.
2. Review the current status for each indicator.
3. Comment to help guide action planning.

Indicator	Current Status	Comment
Example: ■ Big6 Skills are integrated throughout the curriculum	Example: ■ There is a Long Range Curriculum Planning Team that includes classroom teachers, library media specialist, and technology teacher. ■ An analysis of the Curriculum Map shows Big6™ "Bonanza" units in science, social studies, and language arts—grades 6 and 8. Also, strong Big6™ units in science and health—grade 7.	Example: ■ Need to develop or redesign units in art, music, and math—grades 6 through 8

Worksheet 10-4—Big6™ Program Planning Worksheet

	Immediate	Short Term	Long Term
What do I want to have happen?			
How can I make it happen?			
Who can help me and how can they help?			
What will I accept as evidence that I am achieving my goals?			
What will I do tomorrow?			

Putting It All Together

Information & Technology Skills for Student Success: The Big6™ Skills Approach

Summary—Problems

- Information overload
- Information quality
- Student lack of information & technology skills
- Technology out of context

Final Suggestions

- Recognize the challenges of the information age.
- Remember context #1—the information problem-solving process (the Big6™).
- Remember context #2—technology in a Big6™ context.
- Remember context #3—the curriculum or real needs.
- Collaborate: Classroom teachers, administrators, library/info professionals, students, community.

Summary—Solutions

- Process as well as content
- Information and technology literacy
- Context—not an add-on!
  - within the process
  - tied to existing curriculum, instruction, and assignments

1 + 1 + 1 = 1

Classroom Curriculum
\+ Big6
\+ Technology

= Student Achievement!

Think Sheet

Part XI: Supplemental Readings

The BIG6™ Supplemental Readings

This Man Wants to Change Your Job

By Michael B. Eisenberg with Danielle H. Miller
School Library Journal, 9/1/2002

Mike Eisenberg offers a compelling blueprint for becoming a core player in your school.

How can we ensure that students learn essential information skills? How can we partner with teachers to provide meaningful learning opportunities? How can we ensure that school librarians are central players in our schools?

The answers to these key questions lie in creating and managing exemplary library programs. As librarians, it's our job to ensure that administrators, teachers, parents, and decision makers fully comprehend that effective library programs are critical to boosting student learning and achievement.

Of course, changing perceptions is never easy. So we've developed a simple yet powerful strategy that school librarians can use to transform their programs into vibrant elements of a K–12 education. It is as simple as A (Articulate a vision and agenda), B (Be strategic), C (Communicate continuously).

Articulate a Vision and Agenda

The mission statement from *Information Power* (ALA, 1998) sums it up perfectly: The library media program ensures that students "are effective users of ideas and information." That statement defines the school library program's vital role and the importance of teacher-librarians. Refer to it as frequently as possible—in written, verbal, and electronic communication. Include it in the prologue of any report or presentation you distribute, and use it for self-assessment so other teachers understand what you're trying to achieve.

The statement should also frame the library program's most important contributions, or tangible outputs, to student education: information literacy instruction, reading advocacy, and information management. School librarians *teach* meaningful information and technology skills that can be fully integrated with the regular classroom curriculum. They *advocate* reading through guiding and promoting it. And they *manage* information services, technologies, resources, and facilities (see figure 1, below).

Figure 1

Program Function		Role of School Librarian
Information Literacy Instruction	▶	Teacher
Reading Advocate	▶	Advocate
Information Management	▶	Manager

Let's take a more in-depth look at these roles. First and foremost, today's school librarian is a teacher, primarily of information literacy. But the school librarian also partners with classroom teachers. *Information Power* describes this dual role: as a teacher, the school librarian "collaborates with students and other members of the learning community to analyze learning and information needs, locate and use resources that will meet those needs, and to understand and communicate the information the resources provide." As a partner, the school librarian "joins with teachers and others to identify links across student information needs, curricular content, learning outcomes, and a wide variety of print, nonprint, and electronic information resources."

The school librarian also serves as a reading advocate. Reading proficiency is widely recognized as the number-one predictor of student success. In *The Power of Reading: Insights from the Research* (Libraries Unlimited, 1993), education researcher Stephen Krashen says free school reading programs are consistently effective—more than 90 percent of student readers do as well or better than those engaged in traditional language arts programs. Krashen adds that the California Assessment Program (CAP) reports a direct correlation between the amount eighth graders say they read each day and their test scores on the CAP English and language arts test. Furthermore, the "independent learner" part of the *Information Power* standards for student learning states that the pupil "who is an independent learner is information literate and appreciates literature and other creative expressions of information."

The school librarian can run his or her program in collaboration with classroom teachers, reading specialists, and other educators, exciting students about books and media, as well as providing easy access to rich book and media collections. As a reading advocate, school librarians fulfill the teacher and instructional partnership expectations of *Information Power.*

Information management extends beyond building and managing library collections and services. As in many other organizations, each school needs a chief information officer or CIO. The CIO oversees information services, systems, and resources, while delivering information and technology facilities, resources, and services.

The CIO fulfills two roles outlined in *Information Power*: information specialist and program administrator. As an information specialist, the school librarian provides leadership and expertise in acquiring and evaluating all kinds of information; builds collaborative relationships with teachers, administrators, students, and others; and creates strategies for locating, accessing, and evaluating information within and beyond the library media center.

As program administrator, the school librarian works collaboratively with members of the learning community to define policies and guide and direct all related library activities. This requires proficiency in the use of information and information technologies; the ability to provide knowledge, vision, and leadership; and being able to plan, execute, and evaluate the program regularly and on different levels. This vision and agenda have a direct impact on student learning and achievement and ensure that students are effective users of ideas and information.

Be Strategic

Librarians seem to treat "strategic management" as a dirty phrase, something to be avoided or minimized at best. It should be just the opposite: strategic management turns vision into reality. As shown above, our vision is clear. But hard work alone isn't enough. Turning the vision of the school library program into reality requires two essential elements of good management: strategic thinking and strategic planning.

Strategic thinking is a way to approach problems and opportunities. Effective strategic thinking centers on attitude, insight, and political savvy, as well as flexibility. In many ways, attitude is everything. Success starts with attitude. A positive attitude breeds positive results, a negative one breeds failure. If you think you can't make something happen, chances are you won't. If you think you can, at least you have a fighting chance. Attributes of a positive attitude include passion, enthusiasm, optimism, and energy. Successful school librarians are often characterized by their positive can-do attitudes.

I'm not suggesting that school librarians be overly optimistic. Schools and libraries face changing demands, not to mention financial difficulties. But it's time to stop whining. Instead, start spreading the message that school library programs promote student achievement and well-being.

Insight and political savvy mean recognizing and taking advantage of opportunities, connecting with key players, and being seen as a positive and vital force within the school. Your library program must also have a direct link to school initiatives, concerns, and priorities (see figure 2 on page 198 for some key questions to consider and actions to take).

Being politically savvy also means involving others in decision making. Create a formal library advisory committee composed of a key administrator and two or three classroom teachers who are "movers and shakers." Others, such as parents, technology or curriculum coordinators, and students, may be added.

A library advisory committee reinforces the view that the library isn't the personal domain of the school librarian—it belongs to everyone in the school community. A library advisory committee also provides a support base for the library program and librarian. Not only do its members lend clout, but it also creates a mechanism for setting priorities, troubleshooting, and long-term planning.

Figure 2

Key Questions	Library Program Actions
What are the school's key concerns, programs, and initiatives?	■ Link the three functions (information literacy instruction, reading advocacy, information management) to addressing concerns, supporting programs, and fulfilling initiatives. ■ Frame the library program in terms of where the action is (for example, information and technology, performance, and achievement). ■ Recognize that concerns, programs, and initiatives change—sometimes from year to year.
Who are the movers and shakers in the school?	■ Involve them in decision making about the library program.
Who's respected?	■ Help them to succeed in achieving their goals and priorities.
Who gets things done?	■ Ally yourself with winners.
How do things really get done in school, not necessarily the "official" ways, but the real ways—particularly in terms of priority setting, budget and spending, and decision making?	■ Align the management processes of the library program to the processes of the school. ■ Be seen as part of the solution, not part of the problem.

The library advisory committee should meet regularly to:

- Advise on the broad program.
- Set priorities for the library program.
- Help the librarian and staff determine where to spend most of their time and effort.
- Troubleshoot immediate problems.
- Engage in long-term problem solving and planning for major objectives and concerns.
- Establish policies.

Flexibility is central to strategic thinking. There are few absolutes in education: program needs and priorities change from year to year. This year, for example, your school's focus may be on improving reading scores through coordinated schoolwide efforts. This would likely call for an increased emphasis on your role as a reading advocate, while maintaining or perhaps reducing activities related to information literacy instruction or information management. Next year, however, the school may focus on integrating technology into classrooms, and the library program will have to shift its emphasis accordingly. The library advisory committee can play a very useful role in these decisions, as well as getting the message out to the rest of the school.

Strategic planning deserves an article in itself, but here are a few core elements to focus on: a systems approach; analysis and planning; and implementation and documentation of outputs.

A systems approach means looking at an organization in terms of inputs, processes, and outputs. For example, inputs refer to the building blocks of the library program — the staff, resources, information technology systems, facilities, and budget. Outputs are the services, instruction, and resources that the program provides to students and faculty. When describing their programs, librarians frequently focus on the inputs when they should be promoting the outputs. Decision makers don't care so much about inputs. They're more interested in the results — what programs provide for students.

The three main outputs of a library program are instruction, reading advocacy, and information management. They can be subdivided even further, for example, into information and technology skills instruction, reading guidance activities, and information services, facilities, and collection services.

Processes turn inputs into outputs. They include analysis, decision making, implementation strategies, planning, managing, and communication. Formal processes are critical to achieving the ultimate output — getting students to become effective users of ideas and information.

Analysis and planning are crucial. Analyze what is currently real, what is desired, and then plan how to get there. Once the analysis is complete, implement a rolling five-year plan to get the desired results. This plan starts with specific objectives and shifts to a more general plan projecting into the future. The whole point is to make planning an ongoing process that requires continuous revision and reevaluation. A rolling plan does not imply never reaching one's goals. In fact, you should be able to look back at any period and determine whether your original objectives, steps, and goals were attained. Finally, some points about implementation and documentation of outputs. Many school librarians don't adequately document the activities of their library programs. Anecdotal information is not enough. The name of the game is accountability. If any data collection and reporting is done, it's usually based on inputs: size of the collection, numbers of books and other materials (including computers), or the facility itself. Usually, circulation statistics are the only output-oriented numbers reported. Circulation statistics, however, only tell a very small part of the library program story—and sometimes a misleading one. In many secondary schools, for example, book circulation is low simply because most students use electronic and periodical resources—not because they don't read. Remember, the library program centers on three primary activities: information literacy instruction, reading advocacy, and information management. These are the areas that need to be documented with clear evidence of what the program is doing (see figure 3 for an example of how to document your teaching efforts).

Documenting Your Teaching Efforts

- ⊠ Actual Information literacy lesson.
- ☒ Actual Information is touched upon.
- ☐ No Information literacy lesson.

GR	TCHR	UNIT	SUBJECT	ASSIGNMENT1	QTR	1 Task Definition	2 Information Seeking Strategies	3 Location and Access	4 Use of Information	5 Synthesis	6 Evaluation	COMMENTS
6	SEB	Current Events	Social Studies	Report	1 2 3 4	⊠	⊠	⊠	⊠	⊠	⊠	Addresses all Big6 skills year around.
6	ARB	Poetry	English	Short Written Assignment	4	☐	☐	☐	⊠	⊠	⊠	Encourage students to write creative poems.
7	MET	Graphs	Math	Product Assignment	2	☐	☐	☐	⊠	⊠	☐	Emphasizes various graphs and spreadsheet software.
7	TCH	Recycling	Social Studies	Product	2 3	⊠	⊠	⊠	☒	⊠	☒	Introduces technology.
8	HJW	Map Skills	Social Studies	Worksheet	1	☐	⊠	☐	⊠	☐	☐	Teaches how to use maps.
8	TMJ	Noise	Science	Written Report	2	☒	⊠	⊠	☐	⊠	☒	Builds on students' understanding of technology.
7-8	CER	Diet and Nutrition	Health	Posters	1 3	⊠	⊠	☒	☒	⊠	☒	A comprehensive health unit offered twice a year.
7-8	CER	Tobacco and Nutrition	Health	Test	1 3	⊠	☐	☐	⊠	⊠	⊠	Reinforces an understanding of the dangers of smoking.

Adapted from The New Improved Big6 Workshop Handbook *(Linworth, 1999).*

Communicate Continuously

Let's face it, school librarians do a poor job of getting the word out about the importance of their library programs. It's critical for your principal and administration to fully embrace the vision of an active, engaged library program. Much more can be accomplished when you have the support of the entire school community.

A memo to the principal is a nice way to keep the administration apprised of the value, progress, and future of your program. A memo will enlighten the principal and others of the important work you're doing with student learning. It should also emphasize the Information Power vision to ensure that students are effective users of ideas and information.

In your memo, describe the library program's major accomplishments for the year. Use an introductory sentence or two and then bullet or highlight the library's programs in terms of:

- Learning and teaching.
- Information access and delivery.
- Program administration.

Then emphasize the following outputs (teaching and other services):

- Information and technology literacy efforts.
- Information literacy standards.
- How they were integrated with classroom learning.
- Their quantitative impact on learning (i.e., number of classes and students taught).
- Reading advocacy efforts.
- Role of technology, including the Internet, networks, and other tools.

You can also supplement your regular communications by setting up a Web site with quarterly updates and highlights on your and your students' accomplishments. Consider putting together an online discussion group for administrators and parents.

Make sure this vision is embraced by students, administration, other teacher-librarians, and parents. And meet with them regularly. Make the task of producing information-literate students a community-wide challenge.

By embracing this vision and strategy, we can transform library programs and the role of the librarian. Remember, be active and engaged: you are an information literacy teacher, reading advocate, and chief information officer. Think strategically and politically. By taking a systematic approach, you will not only improve your own program, but also gain attention and widespread support. Wherever you are, and to whomever you speak, make sure you communicate the vision of the 21st-century teacher-librarian.

Author Information

Michael B. Eisenberg is dean of the Information School of the University of Washington in Seattle. Danielle H. Miller is an assistant to the dean and a student in the Master of Library and Information Science program at the university.

Reprinted with permission. Eisenberg, M.B., & Miller, D.H. (2002),. This Man Wants to change your job. *School Library Journal, 48*(9), p.46-50.

Acing the Exam

By Rick Margolis
School Library Journal, 10/1/2002

How can librarians boost students' test scores? Bob Berkowitz shares a strategy for success.

Bob Berkowitz is tackling one of his favorite topics, high-stakes tests — those thorny competency-based exams that many students must pass before receiving their high school diplomas. As the accountability movement in American education continues to swell, an increasing number of states, including Connecticut, Texas, Michigan, and New York, have turned to formal assessments to gauge students' understanding of such disparate subjects as history, biology, language arts, physics, math, and foreign languages. In the anxiety-laden realm of big-time testing, Berkowitz is the equivalent of Mr. Goodwrench, seemingly able to fix whatever ails struggling students and perplexed instructors. In short, he's a school librarian who knows how to help kids become more sophisticated thinkers and, by extension, more savvy test takers.

The secret of Berkowitz's success is embodied in the Big6™, a generic problem-solving strategy that he and his colleague Mike Eisenberg, now dean of the University of Washington's School of Information, invented in the late 1980s. The Big6™ approach, as its name suggests, distills the decision-making process into six discrete, interrelated skills: task definition, information-seeking strategies, location and access, use of information, synthesis, and evaluation. (For more details, visit <www.big6.org>.)

The 54-year-old Berkowitz, a library media specialist at Wayne Central High School in Ontario Center, NY, is an unabashed Big6™ booster — and for good reason. Five years ago, for example, he helped transform Scott Hopsicker, a fledgling social studies teacher at Wayne Central High, into an instructional dynamo. At the time, Hopsicker's students had performed poorly on New York's American History Regents Examination: for two consecutive years, scarcely more than 50% scraped by. Yet after working with Berkowitz, an impressive 91% of his class sailed successfully through the test. More recently, Berkowitz has had similar results in the sciences, helping teacher Mike Carges prime his Wayne Central students for the advanced placement test in physics. We spoke to Berkowitz about how librarians can play a leading role in helping students excel on tough formal tests.

Describe your approach to improving students' test scores.

The [most important] thing for me is this notion that instruction is a series of information problems — a very empowering idea for school librarians. What it says is that if you have an information problem-solving model as your curriculum, then you can use that model to design instruction and to teach skills so that students engage the content. Whenever you have a problem to solve or a decision to make, you can use this approach. It doesn't matter whether you're interested in finding out if whales swim on their backs, if chickens have elbows, what movie you want to go to on Friday night, or if it's the right time to refinance your mortgage.

Talk about working with teacher Scott Hopsicker.

Scott is a highly motivated young teacher. We analyzed the Regents Examination and the curriculum. We also looked at his prior teaching strategy, his approach to teaching. We had to develop a collaborative relationship, things that we believed in together. For example, we brainstormed on the characteristics that were indicative of high-quality instruction. We wanted to move students from being dependent learners to being independent learners. We wanted students to be able to incorporate higher-order thinking skills, because the examinations at the end [of the year] require analysis, synthesis, and evaluation. [The exams] also require being able to move from literal to interpretive to applied levels of thinking. We wanted to incorporate [those critical thinking skills] into our instructional models.

What we found was that in the prior year when we looked over the way he taught and his instructional materials and reviewed his lesson-plan book, we discovered that he was teaching a lot of content and [neglecting] the [problem-solving] processes needed to engage that content.

Is that characteristic of most teachers?

I think that most teachers approach instruction that way. So we taught kids how to think like social scientists. Right or wrong, we decided that we were going to teach social studies as a cause-and-effect relationship between social, political, and economic [factors] and foreign affairs.

Can you give an example of what an emphasis on process, rather than content, looks like in the classroom?

One of the early assignments was a fairly traditional assignment. It was to have students make a salt map of a country that had geographic features. We had students look at the impact of rivers on social, political, economic, and foreign affairs. The impact of mountains on social, political, economic, and foreign affairs. The impact of deserts on social [events]. In other words, what's the cause-and-effect relationship of geography to this discourse. Many of these [high-stakes] exams — the Regents exam and the state competency kinds of exams — are quite willing to give students information. But what they're asking students is to use those higher-order thinking skills — analysis, interpretation, the application of information — to solve a problem or answer a question.

In the elementary school, the cue words that lead you to this notion of problem solving [are] "who," "what," "when," "where," "why," [and] "how." Those are cue words to knowing that you have a problem to solve or a decision to make. In a secondary [education] situation, those morph or change into [words] like "compare" and "contrast" and "evaluate," "analyze," "discuss." Those are all, in effect, the first words to questions on the examinations.

I encouraged him to use these kinds of questions in his teaching to move students toward a higher order of thinking. He began asking questions: "What are the relationships between?" "How does this compare to?" "What is the effect on?" "How would this change if?" He moved his questioning techniques from the literal level to this interpretative and applied thinking level. That was real hard for him.

Talk more about the nuts and bolts of making your approach work with teachers.

[Scott and I] invested a lot of time and energy into designing instruction from the perspective that I've outlined. We met formally at least twice a week for two 50-minute planning periods. Additionally, I might have spent another hour working on some aspect of a project that we were collaborating on. He might have spent two or three or [as much as] six hours during the week working on projects, designing his instruction, and then bringing that information back the next time [we met]. We were continually working on instructional activities and units, continually talking about theory and approach. As we got toward the third quarter and fourth quarter [of the school year], he became more knowledgeable, more sophisticated: one of my goals was to make him an independent Big6er. Over time, the amount of time we spent together decreased. He became more competent.

What are some of the specific ways you collaborated with him?

I did a number of things. I observed his class as a mentor. I did a little bit of co-teaching with him. I did a lot of instructional design with him. In other words, he and I would jointly design instructional units and activities. It goes back to the notion that on one side [of the learning process] there's this content and on the other side, there's Big6™. Scott knows his content. The problem wasn't that he wasn't teaching the content. The problem was that he wasn't also [initially] teaching the [problem-solving] process. So kids didn't know when to engage the content. If they couldn't, for example, analyze what the question required them to do, which is task definition, they weren't able to engage the content he had taught them. They didn't have the right cue. Or, if they didn't practice self-evaluation, they never knew when they were finished. They didn't know what it took to earn an "A," because Scott hadn't considered the notion of evaluation as being important.

How can the average library media specialist begin replicating your success with Scott?

There are some key ideas in activating this collaborative process with teachers. I think school library media specialists need to take the initiative. They need to meet with administrators. The principal is the instructional leader in the school. The administrator needs to know what your approach is, what your curriculum is, what your goals are. Administrators are interested in student performance, student success, and student achievement.

So you addressed all of those concerns?

Absolutely. And early on when I got here, there was a situation with a faculty person who was teaching advanced placement social studies. His students were doing really poorly on a document-based question that appeared on those exams back in the early '80s. I was able to go in, collaboratively design instructional strategies with this teacher, and the scores improved immensely. All of a sudden, I built a lot of value. There was a lot of credibility to what I was saying. In a period of a few months, the scores changed drastically by doing the same basic things—going over and over and over again—what we were talking about relative to Scott Hopsicker. So taking the initiative, I think, is important.

I also think it's important to identify the teachers that you can work with. You know, sometimes those are the early adopters, sometimes they're your friends. Identifying those people who you can best and most easily work with, so you can build some chits, you build some credit. I start with three questions: What do I want to have happen? How can I make it happen? What am I going to accept as evidence that it's going on? I get really focused on those ideas. Trying to find answers to those three questions is really important to me.

Is there anything else you'd like librarians to know?

It's not that I believe in teaching to the test, because there are a lot of people that talk about teaching to the test. What I'm trying to suggest is that the test is a step on the way to something else. The something else, or goal, is that we want students to become lifelong learners. We want students to be able to analyze, synthesize, and evaluate the events and information that impact their daily lives.

Librarians are in a unique position to help that happen. School library media specialists are the only ones with the unique set of training as information professionals in the schools. That's our bread and butter, that's our raison d'être as information specialists. No one else in the school has that area of expertise. They're all content experts. We have this professional obligation to act as consultants and collaborators in instructional design and development.

Author Information

Rick Margolis is SLJ's news and features editor

Margolis, R. (Oct. 2002). Acing the exam: How can librarians boost student's test scores? *School Library Journal. 48*(10) p. 50-52.

ERIC Clearinghouse on Information
& Technology at Syracuse University
621 Skytop Road, Suite 160
Syracuse, New York 13244
www.ericit.org
EDO-IR-2002-04

ERIC Digest

January 1999 EDO-IR-99-02

Information Literacy

By Eric Plotnik

[This Digest is based on "Information Literacy: Essential Skills for the Information Age" by Kathleen L. Spitzer with Michael B. Eisenberg & Carrie A. Lowe.

Definition of Information Literacy

Although alternate definitions for information literacy have been developed by educational institutions, professional organizations and individuals, they are likely to stem from the definition offered in the *Final Report of the American Library Association (ALA) Presidential Committee on Information Literacy*, "To be information literate, a person must be able to recognize when information is needed and have the ability to locate, evaluate and use effectively the needed information" (1989, p. 1). Since information may be presented in a number of formats, the term information applies to more than just the printed word. Other literacies such as visual, media, computer, network, and basic literacies are implicit in information literacy.

The Evolution of a Concept

The seminal event in the development of the concept of information literacy was the establishment of the ALA Presidential Committee on Information Literacy whose final report outlined the importance of the concept. The ALA Presidential Committee precipitated the formation of the National Forum on Information Literacy, a coalition of more than 65 national organizations, that seeks to disseminate the concept. The development of information literacy in K–12 education began with the publication of *A Nation at Risk* in 1983. This was soon followed by *Educating Students to Think: The Role of the School Library Media Program* (1986), a concept paper outlining the role of the library and the role of information resources in K–12 education. Kulthau's *Information Skills for an Information Society: A Review of Research* (1987) included library skills and computer skills in the definition of information literacy. The American Association of School Librarians' (AASL) 1988 publication, *Information Power: Guidelines for School Library Media Programs*, and its 1998 publication *Information Power: Building Partnerships for Learning* emphasize the notion that the mission of the school library media program is "to ensure that students and staff are effective users of ideas and information."

Information Literacy Research

Three themes predominate in research on information literacy:

- Information literacy is a process. Information literacy skills must be taught in the context of the overall process.
- To be successful, information literacy skills instruction must be integrated with the curriculum and reinforced both within and outside of the educational setting.
- Information literacy skills are vital to future success.

An Economic Perspective

The change from an economy based on labor and capital to one based on information requires information literate workers who will know how to interpret information.

- Barner's (1996) study of the new workplace indicates significant changes will take place in the future. Information technology is decentralizing the work force. The work force will be more diverse and the economy will increasingly be more global. The use of temporary workers will increase. These changes will require that workers possess information literacy skills.
- The SCANS (1991) report identifies the skills necessary for the workplace of the future. Rather than

report to a hierarchical management structure, workers of the future will be required to actively participate in the management of the company and contribute to its success. The workplace will require workers who possess skills beyond those of reading, writing and arithmetic.

National and State Standards

With the passage of the Goals 2000: Educate America Act (1994), subject matter organizations were able to obtain funding to develop standards in their respective subject areas. Information literacy skills are implicit in the National Education Goals and national content standards documents.

- Three of the eight National Education Goals demonstrate the critical nature of information literacy to an information society: Goal 1: School Readiness; Goal 3: Student Achievement and Citizenship; Goal 6: Adult Literacy and Lifelong Learning.
- An analysis of national content standards documents reveals that they all focus on lifelong learning, the ability to think critically, and on the use of new and existing information for problem solving.
- Individual states are creating initiatives to ensure that students attain information literacy skills by the time they graduate from high school. Kentucky (1995), Utah (1996), and California (1994) are but three examples of states that have publications depicting these initiatives.
- National content standards, state standards, and information literacy skills terminology may vary, but all have common components relating to information literacy.

K-12 Education Restructuring

Educational reform and restructuring make information literacy skills a necessity as students seek to construct their own knowledge and create their own understandings.

- Educators are selecting various forms of resource-based learning (authentic learning, problem-based learning and work-based learning) to help students focus on the process and to help students learn from the content. Information literacy skills are necessary components of each.
- The process approach to education is requiring new forms of student assessment. Students demonstrate their skills, assess their own learning, and evaluate the processes by which this learning has been achieved by preparing portfolios, learning and research logs, and using rubrics.

Information Literacy Efforts in K-12 Education

Information literacy efforts are underway on individual, local, and regional bases.

- Imaginative Web based information literacy tutorials are being created and integrated with curriculum areas, or being used for staff development purposes.
- Library media programs are fostering information literacy by integrating the presentation of information literacy skills with curriculum at all grade levels.
- Information literacy efforts are not being limited to the library field, but are also being employed by regional educational consortia.
- Parents are encouraging their children to develop information literacy skills at home by contacting KidsConnect, the Internet help and referral service for K–12 students. Parents are also helping students work through the information problem solving process as they assist their children with their homework.

Information Literacy in Higher Education

The inclusion of information competencies as a graduation requirement is the key that will fully integrate information literacy into the curricula of academic institutions.

- Information literacy instruction in higher education can take a variety of forms: stand-alone courses or classes, online tutorials, workbooks, course-related instruction, or course-integrated instruction.
- State-wide university systems and individual colleges and universities are undertaking strategic planning to determine information competencies, to incorporate instruction in information competence throughout the curriculum and to add information competence as a graduation requirement for students.
- Academic library programs are preparing faculty to facilitate their students' mastery of information literacy skills so that the faculty can in turn provide information literacy learning experiences for the students enrolled in their classes.

Technology and Information Literacy

Information Technology is the great enabler. It provides, for those who have access to it, an extension of their powers of perception, comprehension, analysis, thought, concentration, and articulation through a range of activities that include: writing, visual images, mathematics, music, physical movement, sensing the environment, simulation, and communication (Carpenter, 1989, p. 2).

Technology, in all of its various forms, offers users the tools to access, manipulate, transform, evaluate, use, and present information.

- Technology in schools includes computers, televisions, video cameras, video editing equipment, and TV studios.
- Two approaches to technology in K-12 schools are technology as the object of instruction approach, and technology as the tool of instruction approach.
- Schools are starting to incorporate technology skills instruction in the context of information literacy skills.
- Technology is changing the way higher education institutions are offering instruction.
- The use of the Internet is being taught the contexts of subject area curricula and the overall information literacy process.
- There is some empirical indication that students who use technology as a tool may become better at managing information, communicating, and presenting ideas.

Conclusion

"In this next century, an "educated" graduate will no longer be defined as one who has absorbed a certain body of factual information, but as one who knows how to find, evaluate, and apply needed information" (Breivik, 1998, p.2). Our ability to be information literate depends on our willingness to be lifelong learners as we are challenged to master new technologies that will forever alter the landscape of information.

References

American Association of School Librarians and Association for Educational Communications and Technology. (1988). *Information power: Guidelines for school library media programs.* Chicago: Author. (ED 315 028)

American Library Association and Association for Educational Communications and Technology. (1998). *Information power: Building partnerships for learning.* Chicago: Author.

American Library Association Presidential Committee on Information Literacy. (1989).*Final report.* Chicago: Author. (ED 315 028)

Barner, R. (1996, March/April). Seven changes that will challenge managers-and workers. *The Futurist, 30* (2), 14–18.

Breivik. P. S. & Senn, J. A. (1998). *Information literacy: Educating children for the 21st century.* (2nd ed.). Washington, DC: National Education Association.

Carpenter, J. P. (1989). *Using the new technologies to create links between schools throughout the world: Colloquy on computerized school links.* (Exeter, Devon, United Kingdom, 17–20 Oct. 1988).

Hashim, E. (1986). Educating students to think: The role of the school library media program, an introduction. In *Information literacy: Learning how to learn.* A collection of articles from School Library Media Quarterly, 15 (1), 17–18.

Kuhlthau, C. C. (1987). *Information skills for an information society: A review of research.* Syracuse, NY: ERIC Clearinghouse on Information Resources. (ED 297 740)

National Commission of Excellence in Education. (1983). *A Nation at risk: The imperative for educational reform.* Washington, DC: U.S. Government Printing Office. (ED 226 006)

Secretary's Commission on Achieving Necessary Skills. (1991). *What work requires of schools: A SCANS report for America 2000.* Washington, DC: U.S. Government Printing Office. (ED 332 054)

This Digest was prepared by Eric Plotnick, Associate Director of the ERIC Clearinghouse on Information & Technology.

ERIC Clearinghouse on Information & Technology, Syracuse University, 621 Skytop Rd. Suite 160, Syracuse, New York 13244-4100; (315) 443-3640; (800) 464-9107; Fax: (315) 443-5448; E-mail: eric@ericir.syr.edu; URL: <http://ericit.org>.

This publication is funded in part with Federal funds from the U.S. Department of Education under contract number ED-99-CO-0005. The content of this publication does not necessarily reflect the views or policies of the U.S. Department of Education nor does mention of trade names, commercial products, or organizations imply endorsement by the U.S. Government. The Department of Education's Web address is: <http://www.ed.gov/>.

ERIC Digest

ERIC Clearinghouse on Information & Technology at Syracuse University
621 Skytop Road, Suite 160
Syracuse, New York 13244
www.ericit.org
EDO-IR-2002-04

August 2000 EDO-IR-2000-06

Teachers and Librarians: Collaborative Relationships

By Shayne Russell

Introduction

Since the early 1980s, library literature has examined progress toward establishing successful collaborative relationships between classroom teachers and library media specialists. In 1989, Berkowitz and Eisenberg acknowledged the gap between the library media specialist's potential as a curriculum consultant in theory and in practice, noting that library media specialists' interest in being involved in curriculum dates back to the 1950s. Assignments developed in partnership between teachers and library media specialists are known to be more "authentic"—exhibiting a higher degree of meaning and significance (Gross & Kientz, 1999). When not guided in the use of a process, students tend to approach research as though there is only one right answer, and fail to learn how to use information to construct their own meaning (Kuhlthau, 1995). This ability to construct meaning is at the heart of information literacy, which collectively describes the skills students will need to cope in a complex world with access to an ever increasing wealth of information.

The results of a study by the Library Service Center of the Colorado State Library offer the most recent support for library media specialists and teachers working collaboratively. The study concludes that test scores increase as school librarians spend more time collaborating with and providing training to teachers, providing input into curricula, and managing information technology for the school (Manzo, 2000). A significant number of prior studies also indicate a positive relationship between the library media program and academic achievement. Didier (1984) examines 38 of these studies, including Gaver's (1963) study of the impact of elementary library service on test scores; Greve's (1974) research on the effect of library service on the academic achievement of high school seniors; and Snider's (1965) investigation of the relationship between college success and knowledge of information skills.

Collaboration Defined

Collaboration is based on shared goals, a shared vision, and a climate of trust and respect (Muronago & Harada, 1999). Each partner fulfills a carefully defined role; comprehensive planning is required; leadership, resources, risk, and control are shared; and the working relationship extends over a relatively long period of time (Callison, 1999). The teacher brings to the partnership knowledge of the strengths, weaknesses, attitudes and interests of the students, and of the content to be taught. The media specialist adds a thorough understanding of information skills and methods to integrate them, helping the teacher to develop resource-based units that broaden the use of resources and promote information literacy (Doiron & Davies, 1998). Additional benefits include more effective use of both resources and teaching time, integration of educational technologies, and a reduced teacher/student ratio (Doiron & Davies, 1998). Teachers with experience in collaborative planning and teaching view the role of the library media specialist more positively and welcome continued collaboration. Participants believe that the results of the collaboration are more powerful and significant than the results of their individual efforts (Friend & Cook, 1996).

Conditions Favorable to Collaborative Partnerships

Administrative Factors

Studies of successful collaborative partnerships have helped us to learn more about the factors conducive to this type of relationship. A recognized barrier to successful collaboration is lack of time (Bishop & Larimer,

1999). Library media specialists with flexible schedules are able to devote more time to planning and working with teachers (Callison, 1999). While media specialists on a fixed schedule spend up to five minutes planning with a teacher, a media specialist on a flexible schedule spends more than 30 minutes (Haycock, 1998). Media specialists with flexible schedules also develop four and one-half times as many integrated units of study than do those on fixed schedules, as well as teaching more information skills lessons integrated with classroom instruction (Tallman & van Deusen, 1994). Scheduling common planning time for teachers and media specialists also promotes collaboration. The greatest amount of collaboration occurs when the media specialist has a flexible schedule and team planning is encouraged by the principal (Tallman & van Deusen, 1994).

Several Canadian studies have shown that principals have a better understanding of the school library program and view it more positively than do classroom teachers (Oberg, 1995). Their critical role in promoting collaborative relationships goes beyond scheduling. Principal support includes working directly with teachers to develop their understanding of the role of the library. This is accomplished through staff inservices, featuring library activities in staff meetings, stating expectations of teachers regarding library use both during the hiring process and afterwards, and serving as a role model by effectively using the library and its information literacy program (Oberg, 1995). Administrators who ask how teachers are using the resources of the media center and the expertise of the library media specialist create an atmosphere where collaboration is more likely to occur (Bishop & Larimer, 1999).

Interpersonal Factors

Successful collaboration involves changing both the attitudes toward and expectations of the role of the library media specialist (Wolcott, 1996). Research shows that most students, teachers, and administrators don't perceive library media specialists and media centers as integral to their own success (Hartzell, 1997). Library media specialists are often viewed as storytellers and providers of resources rather than co-teachers who share common goals (Bishop & Larimer, 1999). It is up to the library media specialist to take steps to change this by serving on curriculum committees, attending planning meetings, and sharing ideas for integrating the media center into the curriculum (Bishop & Larimer, 1999).

Likewise, teachers need help to make the transition from independent teaching to collaboration. The library media specialist can help facilitate this change by acting as the change agent, innovator, opinion leader and/or monitor (Haycock, 1999). The qualities of a library media specialist most often mentioned in discussions of collaboration are initiative, confidence, communication skills, leadership qualities, and, above all, the willingness to take risks. Library media specialists must assume partnership and look for opportunities to plan with teachers, rather than waiting to be asked (Callison, 1999). Effective social skills are necessary to realizing the vision of collaboration set forth in *Information Power: Building Partnerships for Learning* (1998). Indeed, cognitive styles have been examined, and library media specialists defined as "field-dependent" were found to engage more frequently in collaborative efforts with classroom teachers regardless of time and resource limitations (Montgomery, 1991). Field-dependent library media specialists were characterized by their interest in people, use of others as a source of reinforcement, focus on socially-oriented subject matter, and preference for working with others. Less outgoing library media specialists should note that in the collaborative relationship, both leadership, and risk are shared.

Continued Commitment to the Goal

Haycock (1999) notes that collaborative program planning and team teaching are complex evolutionary changes which require time- perhaps two to five years-to reach effective levels. In the case of library media specialist/teacher collaboration, the transition has been slow. Although library literature reflects more than two decades of interest in collaborative planning, and library media specialists are well-trained to perform in this capacity, there are still fewer examples of instructional partnerships than might be expected (Haycock, 1999). However, commitment to the goal remains strong. The term "collaboration" is one of the most frequently used terms in *Information Power: Building Partnerships for Learning* (Callison, 1999). "Instructional consultant" has been upgraded to instructional and curriculum "partner," reflecting a collaborative relationship where the teacher and library media specialist are viewed as equal contributors (Muronago & Harada, 1999). The future of the library media program will be shaped by the vision for a student-centered library media program described in this revised document. This vision for the future is based on three central ideas which suggest a framework to support the authentic student learning that is the goal of the successful, student-centered library media program. These central ideas are collaboration, leadership, and technology.

References and Suggested Readings

American Association of School Librarians and Association for Educational Communications and Technology. (1998). *Information power: Building* partnerships for learning. Chicago: Author.

Berkowitz, R., & Eisenberg, M. B. (1989). *The curriculum roles and responsibilities of library media specialists*. ERIC Digest. Syracuse, NY: ERIC Clearinghouse on Information & Technology. (ED 308 880)

Bishop, K., & Larimer, N. (1999, October). Literacy through collaboration. *Teacher Librarian, 27*(1), 15–20.

Callison, D. (1999, January). Keywords in instruction: Collaboration. *School Library Media Activities Monthly, 15*(5), 38-40.

Didier, E. K. (1984). Research on the impact of school library media programs on student achievement: Implications for school library media professionals, (ED 279 340). In MacDonald, F. B. (Ed.), *The emerging school library media program* (pp. 25–44). Englewood, CO: Libraries Unlimited.

Doiron, R., & Davies, J.(1998). *Partners in learning: Students, teachers, and the school library*. Englewood, CO: Libraries Unlimited. (ED 417 721)

Friend, M., & Cook, L. (1996). *Interactions: Collaborative skills for school professionals*. (2nd ed.). White Plains, NY: Longman. (ED 340 688)

Garland, K. (1995). The information search process: A study of elements associated with meaningful research tasks. *School Libraries Worldwide, 1*(1), 41–53. (EJ 516 594)

Gaver, M. V. (1963). *Effectiveness of centralized library service in elementary schools*. (2nd ed.). New Brunswick, NJ: Rutgers University Press.

Greve, C. L. (1974). *The relationship of the availability of libraries to the academic achievement of Iowa high school seniors*. (Doctoral dissertation, University of Denver, 1974).

Gross, J., & Kientz, S. (1999, October). Developing information literacy: Collaborating for authentic learning. *Teacher Librarian, 27*(1), 21–25.

Hartzell, G. (1997). The invisible school librarian. *School Library Journal, 43*(11), 24–29. (EJ 554 171)

Haycock, K. (1998, May). Collaborative cultures, team planning and flexible scheduling. *Emergency Librarian, 25*(5), 28. (EJ 570 639)

Haycock, K. (1999, March). Fostering collaboration, leadership and information literacy: Common behaviors of uncommon principals and faculties. *NASSP Bulletin, 83*(605), 82–87. (EJ 585 580)

Kuhlthau, C. C. (1995). The process of learning from information. *School Libraries Worldwide, 1*(1), 1-12. (EJ 503 404)

Lance, K. C. (1994, May). *The impact of school library media centers on academic achievement*. ERIC Digest. Syracuse, NY: ERIC Clearinghouse on Information & Technology. (ED 372 759)

Manzo, K. K. (2000, March 22). *Study shows rise in test scores tied to school library resources*. Education Week on the Web. [Online]. Available: <http://www.edweek.org/ew/ewstory.cfm?slug=28libe.h19> [2000, August].

McGregor, J. (1994). Analysis of thinking in the research process. *School Libraries in Canada, 14*(2), 4–7.

Montgomery, P. (1991). Cognitive style and the level of cooperation between the library media specialist and classroom teacher. *School Library Media Quarterly,* 19(3), 185–191. (EJ 428 857)

Muronago, K., & Harada, V. (1999, October). Building teaching partnerships: The art of collaboration. *Teacher Librarian, 27*(1), 9–14.

Oberg, D. (1995). *Principal support: What does it mean to teacher-librarians?* [Online]. Available: <http://www.ualberta.ca/~doberg/prcsup.htm> [2000, August].

Snider, F. E. (1965). *The relationship of library ability to performance in college*. (Doctoral dissertation, University of Illinois, 1965).

Tallman, J. I., & van Deusen, J.D. (1994). Collaborative unit planning: Schedule, time and participants. *School Library Media Quarterly, 23*(1), 33–37. (EJ 493 343)

Tallman, J. I., & van Deusen, J. D. (1994). The impact of scheduling on curriculum consultation and information skills instruction. *School Library Media Quarterly,* 23(1), 17–25. (EJ 493 341)

Wolcott, L. (1996). Planning with teachers: Practical approaches to collaboration. *Emergency Librarian,* 23(3), 8. (EJ 518 337)

This ERIC Digest was prepared by Shayne Russell, (srussell@voicenet.com), Library Media Specialist, Mt. Laurel Hartford School.

ERIC Clearinghouse on Information & Technology; Syracuse University, 621 Skytop Road, Suite 160; Syracuse, New York 13244-5290; (315) 443-3640; (800) 464-9107; Fax: (315) 443-5448; E-mail: eric@ericir.syr.edu; URL: <http://ericir.syr.edu/ithome>.

This publication is funded in part with Federal funds from the U.S. Department of Education under contract number ED-99-CO-0005. The content of this publication does not necessarily reflect the views or policies of the U.S. Department of Education nor does mention of trade names, commercial products, or organizations imply endorsement by the U.S. government. The Department of Education's Web address is: <http://www.ed.gov/>.

ERIC

ERIC Digest

ERIC Clearinghouse on Information
& Technology at Syracuse University
621 Skytop Road, Suite 160
Syracuse, New York 13244
www.ericit.org
EDO-IR-2002-04

November 2000 EDO-IR-2000-08

The Role of the School Library Media Specialist in the 21st Century

By Carrie A. Lowe

Information Power: Lessons and Legacy

In 1988, the American Library Association published its monograph about school library media standards, *Information Power*. This publication, along with its follow-up published in 1998, provide an extremely helpful road map to guide educators into the next century. *Information Power* underscores the importance of the role of the library media specialist in producing well-rounded, information literate students.

Information Power does more than offer an inspiring vision of the future of library media specialists in the school. The authors provide standards for information literacy learning, as well as indicators for each standard. These standards create goals for all educators.

Technology and Opportunity

What kinds of technology tools will be available to schools in the near future? Some trends appear clear: we will have more connectivity and technology that is customized to individual needs. Technology will be integrated seamlessly. Processing tools, communication tools, and information tools will be connected with common access mechanisms and interfaces. Clearly, future technology will present a special challenge and opportunity for education.

Library media specialists are part of the solution. As noted, librarians are the original information specialists. We call this "the information perspective," and it means that library media specialists look at curriculum, assignments, and learning in terms of the information resources, processes, and technologies required for student success. Library media professionals have tried to teach students to consider the information resources they need and then to use the appropriate access technology to find resources and information.

Library media specialists have been pioneers in teaching information skills and integrating technology skills into the information problem-solving process. One of the most popular approaches to integrated information and technology skills is the Big6™ approach, developed by Mike Eisenberg and Bob Berkowitz (1988). The Big6™ approach is a six-stage, non-linear model for information problem-solving. The Big6™ and other models of the information process (such as those by Kuhlthau, 1993; Stripling and Pitts, 1988; and Pappas and Tepe, 1995) define the path that students take to solve information problems. When the focus is on the problem-solving aspects of learning, technology assumes its rightful place as a tool.

Challenges for Library Media Specialists

Gary Hartzell, professor of education at the University of Nebraska, refers to library media specialists as "invisible" professionals (1997). He argues that in many school districts, library media specialists should be participants in the decisions affecting technology, curriculum, and resources at the school and district level. He also points to the widespread trend of cutting library budgets and, in some cases, library media positions to ease school financial problems.

Hartzell points out that there are very few courses in any major school of education in this country that focus on the use of library and information in learning and teaching. Few teacher-training programs mention the roles of the library media program and the library and information professional at all. Some library media specialists are reluctant to promote themselves to fellow educators and the school administration because they do not clearly communicate the nature and role of library and information work.

Library media specialists need to do a better job of clearly articulating their roles in preparing students for the information- and technology-rich workplace of the future. It is essential for library media specialists to commit themselves to the central principles that define their roles as information specialists and educators — helping students to achieve optimum use of information literacy.

Guiding Principles

- **Principle One: School libraries have no boundaries.** The "library" is not a place; rather, library is everywhere. This means that school library media specialists should not be cloistered within the walls of the library and within the constraints of scheduled library time. Beyond the school environment, students will need to make library skills part of their daily lives. Information problem-solving skills help students on a daily basis.
- **Principle Two: Library and information professionals should be flexible.** In the opening chapter of *Information Power: Building Partnerships for Learning*, the authors describe a vision of the library media specialist in the information-rich society of the future. In their view, library media specialists of the future will need to wear many professional hats. These roles include four basic categories: teacher, instructional partner, information specialist, and program administrator (1998).
- **Principle Three: Ensure that students are effective users of ideas and information.** This principle describes the central vision of Information Power. This is also one of the central tenants of the library profession. Additionally, it highlights the most important and enduring role that the library media specialist plays within the school — that of the provider of information services and skills instruction. All members of the school community need to understand that the library media specialist is uniquely qualified, valuable, and able to provide essential information literacy instruction and valuable information services.
- **Principle Four: Information is everywhere, essential, and central.** Principle Four and Principle One are closely related. Information resources exist inside and outside the library. Students need to master the information literacy skills they will use in everyday life. The idea that information is everywhere is a basic premise of information literacy (Spitzer, Eisenberg & Lowe, 1998).

Change and the Library Media Specialist

The changing role of technology in education will increase opportunities for information literacy educators. As technology becomes more prevalent in learning and teaching, there is even a greater need for information, library, and technology work in schools.

The word "disintermediation" is discussed in reference to future technologies. Disintermediation is the idea that as technology becomes more advanced, users will no longer require assistance to use it (Gillian, 1996). The development of the World Wide Web has revealed a very different story. We have seen a dramatic increase in the use of question-and-answer services (such as AskERIC, <www.askeric.org>) in the past five years. As the Web becomes more complex, users need more help to find what they want. Information and technology specialists are well equipped to help users find information.

The Information and Technology Team

Of course, the roles and responsibilities of the school faculty will also change in the future. Information and technology teams composed of technology teachers, library and information professionals, English teachers, history teachers, and key administrators can help with successful integration of technology. These team members represent the political muscle, technical savvy, and information literacy expertise to ensure that all students get the information literacy instruction they need.

The work of the information and technology team goes beyond creating technology-rich learning environments for students, although this is one of the team's most important tasks. Effective teams have a close relationship with classroom teachers and administration, and their responsibilities affect every aspect of the school. Teams provide a technical support system, coordinate tech services and resources, and facilitate purchasing decisions. The team oversees the information and technology literacy program and ensures it is implemented as part of the classroom curriculum. An active, dynamic information and technology team is an integral part of the school, and they provide essential support to many administrators, teachers, and students.

Where Do We Go from Here?

Educators must assume a leadership role to ensure students learn. But how can we make this vision a reality? Here are a few steps for library media specialists to consider in creating a promising future:

- Learn and absorb. Read and learn about information literacy and share that knowledge with other colleagues.
- Get involved. Become actively involved in the information and technology program. Other teachers, administrators, and parents need to become aware of the importance of library media efforts to help students learn essential skills.

- Be a leader. Assume an active role in decision-making and planning. Become involved with your school's technology committee, and come to meetings with your own vision of what the school's technology policy should contain.

These efforts are not optional. As educators, it is our responsibility to equip our students with the skills and understanding they will need. Clearly, this task will require high-quality library and information technology programs to meet students' needs in schools or in electronic, networked, or virtual learning environments.

Sources

American Association of School Librarians and Association for Educational Communications and Technology. (1988). "Information power." Chicago: American Association of School Librarians.

American Association of School Librarians and Association for Educational Communications and Technology. (1998). "Information power: Building partnerships for learning." Chicago: American Association of School Librarians.

American Library Association Presidential Committee on Information Literacy. (1989). "Final Report." Chicago: Author. (ED 316 074)

Caffarella, E. (1998). The new information literacy standards for student learning: Where do they fit with other content standards? In: "SITE 98: Society for Information Technology & Teacher Education International Conference" (9th, Washington, DC, March 10-14, 1998). Proceedings (ED 421 076).

Eisenberg, M. B., & Berkowitz, R. E. (1988). "Curriculum initiative: An agenda and strategy for library media programs." Greenwich, CT: Ablex. (ED 296 731)

Gillian, A. (1996). Disintermediation: A disaster or a discipline? In: Online Information 96. Proceedings of the International Online Information Meeting (20th, Olympia 2, London, England, United Kingdom, December 3-5, 1996). (ED 411 809).

Hartzel, G. (1997). The invisible school librarian: Why other educators are blind to your value. "School Library Journal," 43(11), 24-29. (EJ 554 171)

Haycock, K. (Ed.). (1998). "Foundations for effective school library media programs." Englewood, CO: Libraries Unlimited. (ED 428 776).

Kuhlthau, C. (1993). "Seeking meaning: A process approach to library and information services." Greenwich, CT: Ablex Publishing Company.

Lighthall, L., Ed.; Haycock, K., Ed. (1997). "Information rich but knowledge poor? Emerging issues for schools and libraries worldwide." Research and Professional Papers Presented at the Annual Conference of the International Association of School Librarianship Held in Conjunction with the Association for Teacher-Librarianship in Canada (26th, Vancouver, British Columbia, Canada, July 6-11, 1997). (ED 412 942).

National Board for Professional Teaching Standards. (2001, in press). "Library Media Standards." Arlington, VA: Author.

Pappas, M., & Tepe, A. (1995). Preparing the information educator for the future. "School Library Media Annual" (SLMA), 13, 37-44. (EJ516 579)

Spitzer, K. (1999). Information literacy: Facing the challenge. "Book Report," 18(1), 28-28. (EJ 589 883).

Spitzer, K., Eisenberg, M. B., & Lowe, C. A. (1998). "Information literacy: Essential skills for the information age." Syracuse, NY: ERIC Clearinghouse on Information & Technology. (ED 427 780)

Stripling, B., & Pitts, J. (1988). " Brainstorms and blueprints: Teaching library research as a thinking process." Littleton, CO: Libraries Unlimited.

This ERIC Digest was prepared by Carrie A. Lowe (calowe@u.washington.edu).

This publication is funded in part with Federal funds from the U.S. Department of Education under contract number ED-99-CO-0005. The content of this publication does not necessarily reflect the views or policies of the U.S. Department of Education nor does mention of trade names, commercial products, or organizations imply endorsement by the U.S. government. The Department of Education's Web address is: <http://www.ed.gov/>.

Reading Advocacy: Creating Contagious Enthusiasm for Books and Reading K–12

By Michael B. Eisenberg

What's this? Mike Eisenberg is writing an article on books, literature, and reading? Is this that Mike Eisenberg? you know, Big6™ Mike Eisenberg? Is it information technology (IT) Mike Eisenberg and the Mike Eisenberg who writes about library media program management and planning? What's going on? Has Mike finally seen the light?

Well yes, it is that same Mike Eisenberg, and no, Mike hasn't finally seen the light because he always saw it. It's a little known fact that as a building-level library media specialist in the 1970s, Mike wrote his very first article for publication—and it was on the topic of booktalking for teens (Eisenberg, 1978). Furthermore, for many years, one of Mike's mainstay teaching assignments at Syracuse University was "Media for Young Adults."

So, don't turn the page; read on and see what Mike has to say in this first of three articles on the roles of the 21st century teacher-librarian.

—Carol Simpson

Introduction: The Mission and Roles of Library Media Programs and Teacher-Librarians

To me, it's really quite simple: it all stems from the mission statement of the library media program from *Information Power*:

> "The mission of the library media program is to ensure that students . . . are effective users of ideas and information."
> (AASL/ACET, 1988, 1998)

Read this statement carefully a couple of times. Turn it over in your mind and think about what it means and the implications for library media programs and the professionals who run them, teacher-librarians (aka library media specialists).

What I like best about this mission statement is that it's bold and ambitious—"the mission ... is to ensure." Wow, that's powerful. No wishy-washy-ness here. We're not talking about facilitating, helping, guiding, encouraging, or assisting. Library media programs and teacher-librarians need to step up to the plate.

And, what is it that we are ensuring? We are ensuring that students are effective users of two things: ideas and information.

Let's start with the latter—"effective users of information" because it's straightforward in terms of implications for library media programs and teacher-librarians. Ensuring that students are effective users of information calls for the library media program to fulfill a teaching role. Teacher-librarians have a clear instructional mandate—to ensure that all students gain the requisite knowledge and skills in order to use information and technology effectively.

While the next article in this series will focus on the teaching role and how to fulfill this role in more depth, let me point out a few key aspects here. First, the charge is to teach all essential information and technology skills. We're not just talking about "library skills" or even "research skills." Students must learn to use the full range of information problem-solving skills. Bob Berkowitz and I have explained these in terms of the Big6™ approach, but others have done so as well (e.g., Kuhlthau, 1993; Pappas, 2001). Second, students should be able to apply information and technology skills across situations, not simply write papers or reports or projects. Information Power doesn't say, "ensure that students are effective users of information for papers and reports." It doesn't even say "in school" or "in the library." This broadens the scope of the charge to library media programs and professionals. We must ensure that students are effective across settings—afterschool, home, recreation—as well as library and classroom.

It is through books and reading that students become effective users of ideas. Library media programs enrich curriculum through literature and motivate students through reading promotion activities.

Lastly, we know that the most effective way to implement the information and technology skills instruction program is through integration with subject area curriculum and through collaboration with classroom teachers, or, information in context. But, let's not forget that this is a *means*, not an end. The ultimate measure of success of the library media program is not the degree to which there is collaboration with classroom teachers; it's whether or not students are effective users of information.

OK, enough on information and technology teaching for now. Let's back up to the other part of the mission statement: to ensure that students are effective users of *ideas*. Again, if you consider this statement carefully, you'll realize that it too is bold, broad, and ambitious. Certainly, one could say that the role of every teacher, regardless of setting or specialization, is to ensure that students are effective users of ideas. But, I think the statement makes a very unique and powerful connection for teacher-librarians because it directly relates to our traditional efforts to promote books and reading. That's because it is through books and reading that students become effective users of ideas. Library media programs enrich curriculum through literature and motivate students through reading promotion activities.

Reading Advocacy: Bold and Active

Take a moment and ponder "books." What is it about books that is so special and unique? Through books, students travel beyond their own environment, across our world as well as to worlds beyond. The book is the original virtual reality technology. Books challenge students to think and to imagine, to wrestle with ideas, and to dream. Our goal as teacher-librarians is to get kids excited about reading, books, and media for two major reasons: (1) reading is the baseline skill for success in all human endeavor, and (2) through reading students learn, grow, and develop.

Reading proficiency is widely recognized as the No. 1 predictor of student success. From *The Power of Reading: Insights from the Research* by Stephen Krashen: "in-school free reading programs [or voluntary reading] are consistently effective. In 39 out of 41 comparisons (93%), readers do as well or better than students who were engaged in traditional language arts programs" (pp. 3). "The California Assessment Program (CAP) reported a clear positive relationship between the amount eighth graders said they read per day and their scores on the CAP test of English and Language Arts. These tests cover reading comprehension; both "basic skills" and "critical thinking"; as well as writing (punctuation, word choice, sentence style, paragraph development)" (pp. 6). This is also included in the "independent learner" part of the *Information Power* standards for student learning that states "[t]he student who is an independent learner is information literate and appreciates literature and other creative expressions of information."

Reading proficiency is widely recognized as the No.1 predictor of student success.

As noted by Cullinan (2000), many teachers of language arts, recognizing the value of independent reading, immerse students in real literature from their earliest encounters with print and establish sustained silent reading time in their classrooms. Cullinan, citing Anderson, Fielding, and Wilson (1988), says students who begin reading a book in school are more likely to continue to read outside of school than students who do not begin a book in school. However, research also suggests that some teachers are not knowledgeable about children's literature; they are not able to introduce students to the wealth of books available, and they may not recognize the effects of their teaching methods on students' attitudes toward reading (Short and Pierce, 1990).

Clearly, a key role for the library media program and teacher-librarian is to advocate books and reading. And, not just for K–8. The mission doesn't stop at the high school doors. The implementation may change, but the role remains the same.

Regardless of grade level, reading advocacy is not an easy task today. Students face lots of distractions including television, computer games, movies, the Web, e-mail, and instant messaging. There are also sports, family, hobbies, and, oh, yes, school. That's right, school too can be a distraction from books and reading because it gobbles up time, effort, and energy. Just ask high school students about how much time they have to read and why they don't read more. They'll tell you it's because they're so busy, and part of that is the busyness of school. And, while we are concerned about shortened attention spans in the classroom, our society seems to be encouraging "multi-processing"—juggling a number of things at the same time. All of these make the task of promoting reading difficult, but more important than ever.

So, if teacher-librarians are serious about the reading advocacy role, they need to get organized and active. Passive reading guidance—when students ask for help—just won't cut it. And, simply providing reading appreciation opportunities isn't enough either.

Teacher-librarians need to capture students' imaginations. We need to understand and apply all the tools of student motivation. One of the most effective motivation approaches is the ARCS model, developed by Keller (1987) and applied to the library and information science field by Small (1997) <http://www.ed.gov/databases/ERIC_Digests/ed409895.html> and one of her students, Chemotti (1992). ARCS stands for **A**ttention, **R**elevance, **C**onfidence, and **S**atisfaction, and these four criteria can be applied to any learning situation:

- Attention means gaining and sustaining students' attention. This requires getting students excited, and equally important, keeping their attention over time. This is a definite challenge considering shrinking attention spans. Reading advocacy activities that focus on attention include reading contests, "everyone read the same book" programs, booktalking, and storytelling.

Figure 1: Reading Advocacy Options

***Note:** This is only a partial list of reading advocacy actions. It is not meant to be comprehensive or selective in terms of best or recommended actions.*

Formal Reading/Media Activities

- Reading clubs
- Reading contests
- Everyone reads the same book
- Storytelling
- Booktalking
- Special reading program (e.g., Accelerated Reader)
- Write a diary as a book character
- Theme-based group reading, e.g., "Climb the Glass Hill" Reading Club, based on reading Scandinavian folktales
- Skits based on books
- Puppet shows based on folktales, fairy tales
- "Researchers Incorporated," choose a topic and read to answer questions and receive a "Researchers Incorporated" card or badge
- Poetry Club to memorize a poem a month (voluntary)
- Reading "contests," e.g., challenge a teacher to read a set number of pages or books (Never based on time because it penalizes slower readers)
- Trivia based on novels

Resources and Facilities Provision

- Special reading or media area
- Displays targeted to specific needs or assignments
- Unique collections

Informal Reading/Media Activities

- One-on-one guidance
- Peer reading advisory service
- Collecting and sharing student reviews

- Relevance means directly relating to the students' needs and interests—either school or personal. Relevance is not always apparent, so teacher-librarians can work to make the connection between a reading activity and the student. Booktalking that focuses on books for school assignments is an effective technique for highlighting books relevant to school interests (more on this in the next section). Booktalking or storytelling can also easily be targeted to personal interests.
- Confidence refers to making sure that the students are comfortable with the level of information being presented. First, can they "get it?" Is the presentation or language too sophisticated? Are they able to understand and respond appropriately to what's being presented? Conversely, is the material or approach too simplistic for them? For reading advocacy activities, this means making sure that the books or media presented are at the students' level and also that the students have confidence that they can attain what is being encouraged (e.g., reading a book a week for the next month).
- Satisfaction is a summative criteria that focuses on how the students feel about the reading activity. Was the experience satisfying and was it worth the time and effort devoted to it? Satisfaction is based on both the content of the reading activity as well as the approach.

Motivation as reflected by ARCS should be a prime consideration when deciding on which reading advocacy options to employ (see Figure 1). Being able to respond affirmatively to each of the ARCS criteria will ensure a successful reading advocacy activity. That is, you are guaranteed success if you can say, "yes—the activity grabbed students' attention, was clearly relevant, was at their level of comfort and confidence, and was ultimately satisfying to the students."

All these options (see Figure 1) seek to motivate and guide students to read. The purpose is to get students focused on reading and to keep their interest. My favorite technique is booktalking, which can take many different forms. The next section focuses on one style of booktalking — mine.

Booktalking Eisenberg Style

In one of my past lives, I had the good fortune to be a high school teacher-librarian in a school of 1,500 students. As you can imagine, we built a program that stressed information-skills instruction fully integrated with the subject area curriculum. In one of our library media program planning sessions, we lamented that the fiction collection seemed underutilized; the students didn't seem to be reading very much — especially for pleasure.

If teacher-librarians are serious about the reading advocacy role, they need to get organized and active. Passive reading guidance — when students ask for help — just won't cut it.

So, we decided that promoting reading and books would be a major goal for the year. We started talking to teachers, particularly those in the English Department, and found that students did have a substantial number of outside reading assignments. Ah ha! Clearly, an opportunity. What if we implemented a booktalking program — one where we targeted our talks about books to specific assignments requiring outside reading?

While we didn't know it then, we were analyzing the need and opportunity from the ARCS perspective. The assignment was the relevance part of ARCS, as many students have a specific need for selecting books for reading. Our challenge then was to grab their attention, match books to their confidence levels, and provide a satisfying experience.

So, we surveyed the English Department for specific assignments and scheduled booktalks. After a few of these we hit our groove in terms of structure and format:

- A 20–30 minute booktalk in the classroom.
- Linked to a specific assignment, which was explained and discussed at the beginning of the booktalk, and made sure that we were on the same page as the classroom teacher.
- Selected 15–20 books (or media, if acceptable) that met the criteria of the assignment.
- Talked briefly (2–4 minutes) about each book:
  - Talked about something special about the book. This could be the plot, characters, author, setting, the link to something the students are familiar with (e.g., a television show, current event).
  - Made the link between the book and the assignment.
  - If I was actually unfamiliar with the book, I would say so while explaining why I selected the book (e.g., from a review, familiar with the author, recommendation from someone else, nice cover).
  - If I hadn't read the book, I would say so as it is critical to be straightforward and honest with the students.
  - Students could sign out a book on the spot. In fact, as soon as students indicated that they wanted books, I would stop talking and give books to them. Usually, for the first few books, there were no takers so I passed the books around but they rarely made it around the room. Later in the talk, sometimes all I had to do was hold up a book and a student would want it.

- Set up a display of additional books relevant to the assignment in the library media center.

Again, we found that we could easily cover 15 to 20 books in 30 minutes. Because there were usually more students than 20, that created demand and kept their attention. We stressed that if they hadn't selected a book, there were more on display in the library media center and we were available for additional assistance.

This high school booktalking program really took off! We started with a few teachers in the English Department and it quickly spread to almost all teachers in the department. We then surveyed other departments to see who was or might be able to require students to read outside materials. We found opportunities throughout the school including:

- A social studies teacher who was interested in teaching concepts (e.g., exploration, conflict, war, social welfare) through literature. We jointly planned an assignment and a reading list matching the concepts.
- Two art teachers who were interested in having students read biographies of famous artists. We were able to get full classes interested in Time-Life and other series on artists.
- Coaches who wanted physical education students as well as sports team members to read books about the nuances of a sport, personal fitness, or overcoming challenges.
- The reading specialist who wanted to introduce high interest books-on-tape to students needing special assistance.

Although not required for the booktalk experience, we delivered these booktalks in the classroom because it dramatically extended the library media program throughout the school and also allowed the library media facility to be used for other needs. We arranged for two teachers per period to be scheduled into the library media center to provide supervision, even when a teacher-librarian was available.

At the peak of the program, we averaged one booktalk per day for 180 booktalks in one year. Later, we scaled back a bit because students now knew about us and were able to be given an assignment and directed to the library media center for books on display and one-on-one guidance.

Ensuring Success and Recognition through Systematic Planning and Documentation

The importance of reading advocacy mandates that teacher-librarians carefully plan and document the full scope of the reading advocacy function of the library media program. I recommend that you systematically plan and document in the following ways:

1. Work with administrators and key teachers in the school (preferably through a building-level planning team if it exists) to determine what is already taking place in the school in terms of reading programs. It is important to determine

a baseline, as it is crucial that the reading advocacy actions of the library media program fully integrate with those of the classroom and the reading program.

2. Work with this same group of administrators and key teachers to establish priorities for the nature and scope of the reading advocacy actions of the library media program. Time and effort are limited. Where is the greatest need for library media involvement and what program actions are likely to have the most impact?
3. Plan the reading advocacy program in advance (e.g., monthly, every 10 weeks, or by marking period) by matching classroom and curriculum need to formal reading advocacy activities as much as possible. Document these plans on a chart.
4. Update the chart each week to document what was accomplished and what actually took place. Library media programs have too few output measures of performance. The completed chart is a firm record of the extent of the reading advocacy program.
5. Provide a brief report to the principal, as well as the group of administrators and key teachers every marking period on the reading advocacy program. Briefly review the goals and objectives, describe what the chart shows in terms of activity, outline plans for the next marking period, and raise any issues or concerns.

This approach will raise awareness of the library media program and teacher-librarian role in promoting reading in your school. It also will provide opportunities for buy-in by administrators and teachers and facilitate careful analysis and planning. This is crucial in order to coordinate the library media efforts with others and to maximize impact of time and effort allocated to reading advocacy.

Summary

Reading advocacy is an important and fundamental function of the library media program and the role of the teacher-librarian. However, today's demands on schools and library media programs call for a more highly active and engaged reading advocacy program than ever before. The nature and extent of the reading advocacy program, as well as the time and effort allocated, should be directly tied to the needs and situation of the school. Teacher-librarians can facilitate this by involving key administrators and teachers in the decision making process as well as by systematically planning and documenting the reading advocacy program.

Bibliography

Chemotti, J.T. (June 1992). "From nuclear arms to Hershey's kisses: Strategies for motivating students." *School Library Media Activities Monthly, 8*(10), 34-36.

Cullinan, B.E. (2000). "Independent Reading and School Achievement." *School Library Media Research Online*, Vol. 3. <http://www.ala.org/aasl/SLMR/vol3/independent/independent.html>.

Eisenberg and Miller (September 2002). "This man wants to change your job." *School Library Journal, 48*(9), 46-52.

Keller, J.M. (October 1987). "Strategies for stimulating the motivation to learn." *Performance and Instruction, 26*(8), 1-7.

Kuhlthau, C.C. (Fall 1993). "Implementing a Process Approach to Information Skills: A Study Identifying Indicators of Success in Library Media Programs." *School Library Media Quarterly*; Vol. 22, n1, 11-18.

Pappas, M.L. (October 2001). "Teaching Information Skills: Perspective." *School Library Media Activities Monthly*, Vol. 18, n2, 25-28.

Small, Ruth V. (1997). "Motivation in Instructional Design." *ERIC Digest*, ED409895. ERIC Clearinghouse on Information and Technology Syracuse, New York. <www.ed.gov/ databases/ERIC_Digests/ed409895.html>.

Michael Eisenberg is Dean of the Information School of the University of Washington. With co-author Bob Berkowitz, Mike created the Big6™ approach to information problem-solving, and he has worked with thousands of students as people in public school, business, government, and communities to improve their information and technology skills. All Big6™ publications are available from Linworth Publishing. He can be reached at mbe@u.washington.edu or <www.ischool.washington.edu/mbe>.

Reprinted with permission.

Eisenberg, M. (February, 2003). Reading advocacy: Creating contagious enthusiasm for books and reading K-12. *Library Media Connection*, *21*(5), p. 22.

The Big6 Information and Technology Literacy Workshop

Workshop Evaluation

Presenter's Name:

Workshop Location:

# of Attendees:

Date:

Please rate each area: 3—Very Useful; 2—Somewhat Useful; 1—Not Useful;

3	2	1	Topic
			Content of Presentation
			Flow of Presentation
			Information and Internet statistics
			Information Literacy Learning
			Big6™
			Use of Technology
			Developing a Big6™ Lesson
			Big6™ and Assessment
			Integrating the Big6 into the Curriculum
			Balance between presentation use of the web, interaction
			Overall Workshop Rating.

Parts of this workshop that were very useful:

Improvements for future presentations would be:

Big6™ Associates, LLC
P.O. Box 1
Fayetteville, NY 13066

Index

H

I

J

L

M

N

P

Works Cited

Eisenberg, M. B. , & Berkowitz, R. E. (1996), *Helping with homework: A parent's guide to information problem-solving*. Syracuse, NY: ERIC Clearinghouse on Information & Technology. Available from Linworth Publishing 1-800-786-5017.

More Big6™ Connections for You!

Big6™ Online Discussion Group

Participants share information about successful Big6™ experiences; ask for and provide ideas for lessons and units integrating the Big6™ with subject area curriculum or students' personal interests; present problems and offer solutions; and discuss broader issues related to the use of information and technology in education. Membership is free. Readers receive Big6 eNewsletter announcements.
http://www.big6.com/showarticle.php?id=116

Big6™ eNewsletter

Big6™ eNewsletter authors share how educators (K-16 teacher librarians and classroom teachers) create lessons and activities within the context of Big6™ Skills or Super3 Skills. Quarterly issues include Big6™ Essays and Opinion Pieces, Tips, Big6™ Bulletin Board Ideas, Big6™ lesson plans and more. No subscription is necessary. Written by and for frontline Big6ers in schools! We announce each new issue to members of the Big6™ Online Discussion Group!
http://www.big6.com/showenewscategory.php?volume=E4&issue=2

Big6™ Website

The Big6™ Website *http://www.big6.org* is a rich resource for Big6™ lessons, articles, announcements, games, Big6™ store, polls and just about everything we offer in Big6™! This searchable web site can help you get started and will supply your Big6™ information needs throughout the school year. Updated continuously! Freely available.

Big6™ Kids Website

Big6™ Kids *http://www.big6.com/kids*, contains helpful hints, templates, worksheets, songs, games and fun to help children master essential information problem solving skills. Focused sections meet the needs of students in grades K-2, 3-6, and 7-12. Freely available for students, teachers, and parents who want to know more about the Big6™!

Big6™ Professional Development

Big6™ Online Course

"The Big6™ Skills Approach to Information Problem Solving." Big6™ Basics (3 cr.). Rolling enrollment—start anytime. This course goes beyond traditional library location and access skills to emphasize the Big6™ Skills, a six-step approach to problem-solving that integrates information search and use skills along with technology tools in a systematic process to find, use, apply, and evaluate information to specific needs and tasks. To register by telephone using VISA or Master Card, call 206-543-2310 or 1-800-543-2320 or on the Web at: *http://www.outreach.washington.edu*. Co-developed by Big6™ Associates, LLC and University of Washington Education Outreach (UWEO), Seattle.
http://www.big6.com/showarticle.php?id=353

Big6™ Academy

Go beyond Big6™ Basics with this intensive 2-day Big6™ Seminar. You will learn how to analyze and plan for integrated Big6™ information & technology skills instruction; design and implement—with classroom teachers—specific instructional units and lessons integrating Big6™ information & technology skills learning with subject area/classroom curriculum; document the scope and extent of the Big6™ information & technology skills program; and evaluate the success of your Big6™ initiative. Limited to 30 participants per session. Offered semi-annually. For price and schedule information e-mail: *info@Big6.com*

Big6™ Onsite Workshops

Big6™ Workshops—basics through advanced levels—are available upon request at your location throughout the summer and during the academic year. Contact us for price and availability. For information e-mail: *info@big6.com*